EASY PIANO

BIGGEST POP HITS

1996-1997

Arranged by DAN COATES

Project Manager: Carol Cuellar
Book Design: Ken Rehm

Dan Coates

One of today's foremost personalities in the field of printed music, Dan Coates has been providing teachers and professional musicians with quality piano material since 1975. Equally adept in arranging for beginners or accomplished musicians, his Big Note, Easy Piano and Professional Touch arrangements have made a significant contribution to the industry.

Born in Syracuse, New York, Dan began to play piano at age four. By the time he was 15, he'd won a New York State competition for music composers. After high school graduation, he toured the United States, Canada and Europe as an arranger and pianist with the world-famous group "Up With People".

Dan settled in Miami, Florida, where he studied piano with Ivan Davis at the University of Miami while playing professionally throughout southern Florida. To date, his performance credits include appearances on "Murphy Brown," "My Sister Sam" and at the Opening Ceremonies of the 1984 Summer Olympics in Los Angeles. Dan has also accompanied such artists as Dusty Springfield and Charlotte Rae.

In 1982, Dan began his association with Warner Bros. Publications - an association which has produced more than 400 Dan Coates books and sheets. Throughout the year he conducts piano workshops nation-wide, during which he demonstrates his popular arrangements.

Contents

SAY YOU'LL BE THERE

Words and Music by
SPICE GIRLS
and ELIOT KENNEDY
Arranged by DAN COATES

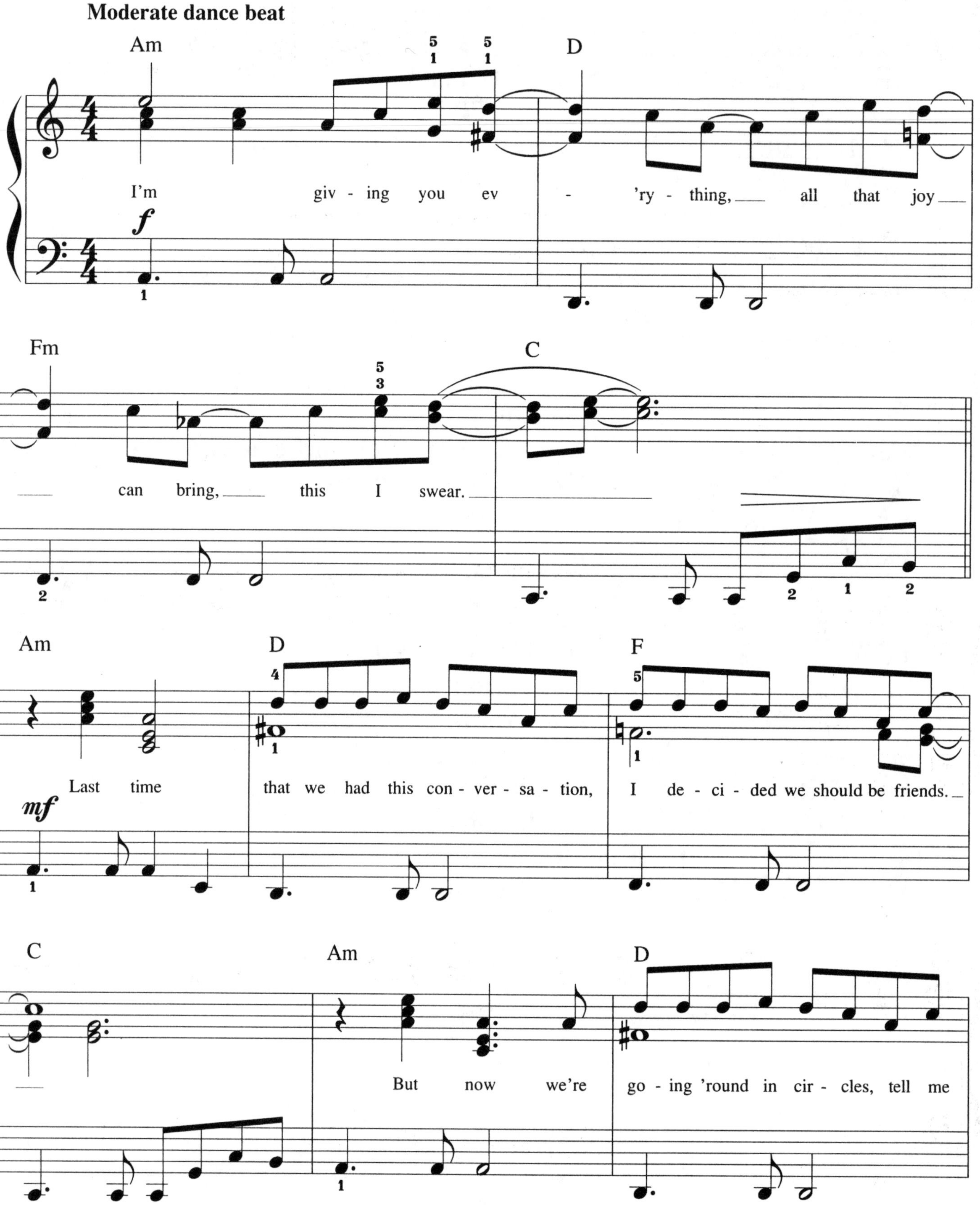

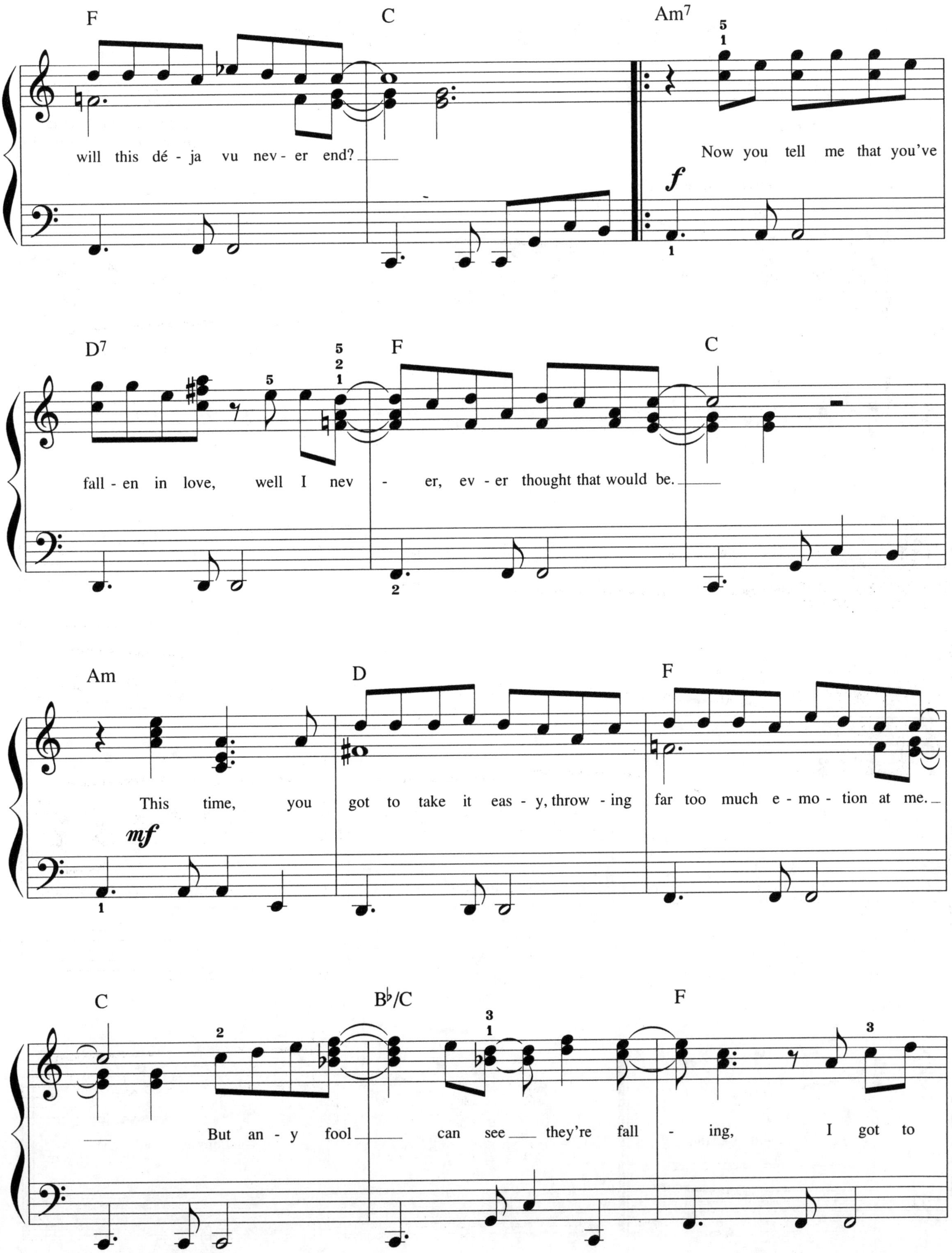
F C Am7
will this déja vu never end?
Now you tell me that you've
f
D7 F C
fall - en in love, well I nev - er, ev - er thought that would be.
Am D F
This time, you got to take it eas - y, throw - ing far too much e - mo - tion at me.
mf
C B♭/C F
But an - y fool can see they're fall - ing, I got to

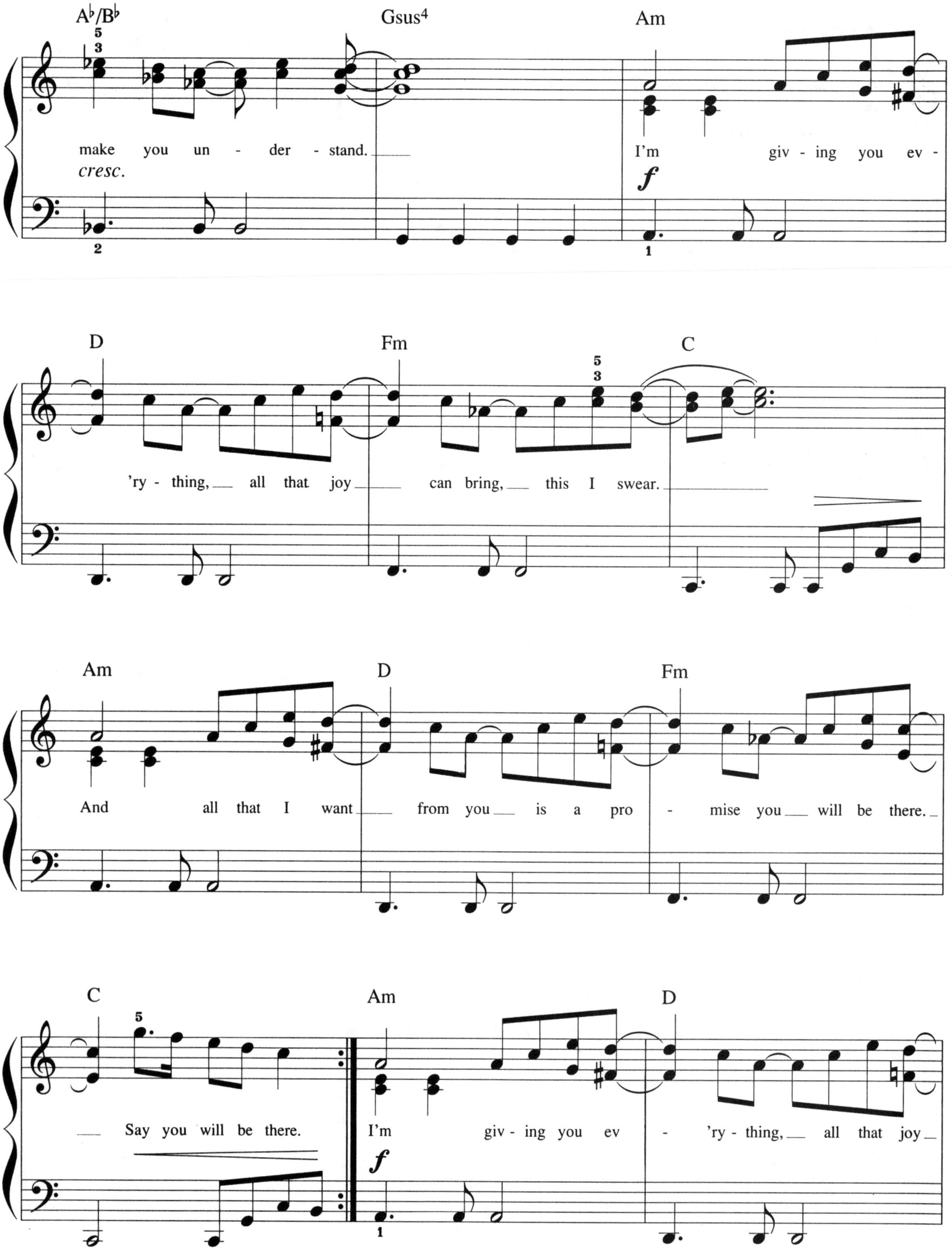
A♭/B♭
Gsus4
Am
make you un - der - stand.
I'm giv - ing you ev -
cresc.
f
D
Fm
C
'ry - thing, all that joy can bring, this I swear.
Am
D
Fm
And all that I want from you is a pro - mise you will be there.
C
Am
D
Say you will be there.
I'm giv - ing you ev - 'ry - thing, all that joy
f

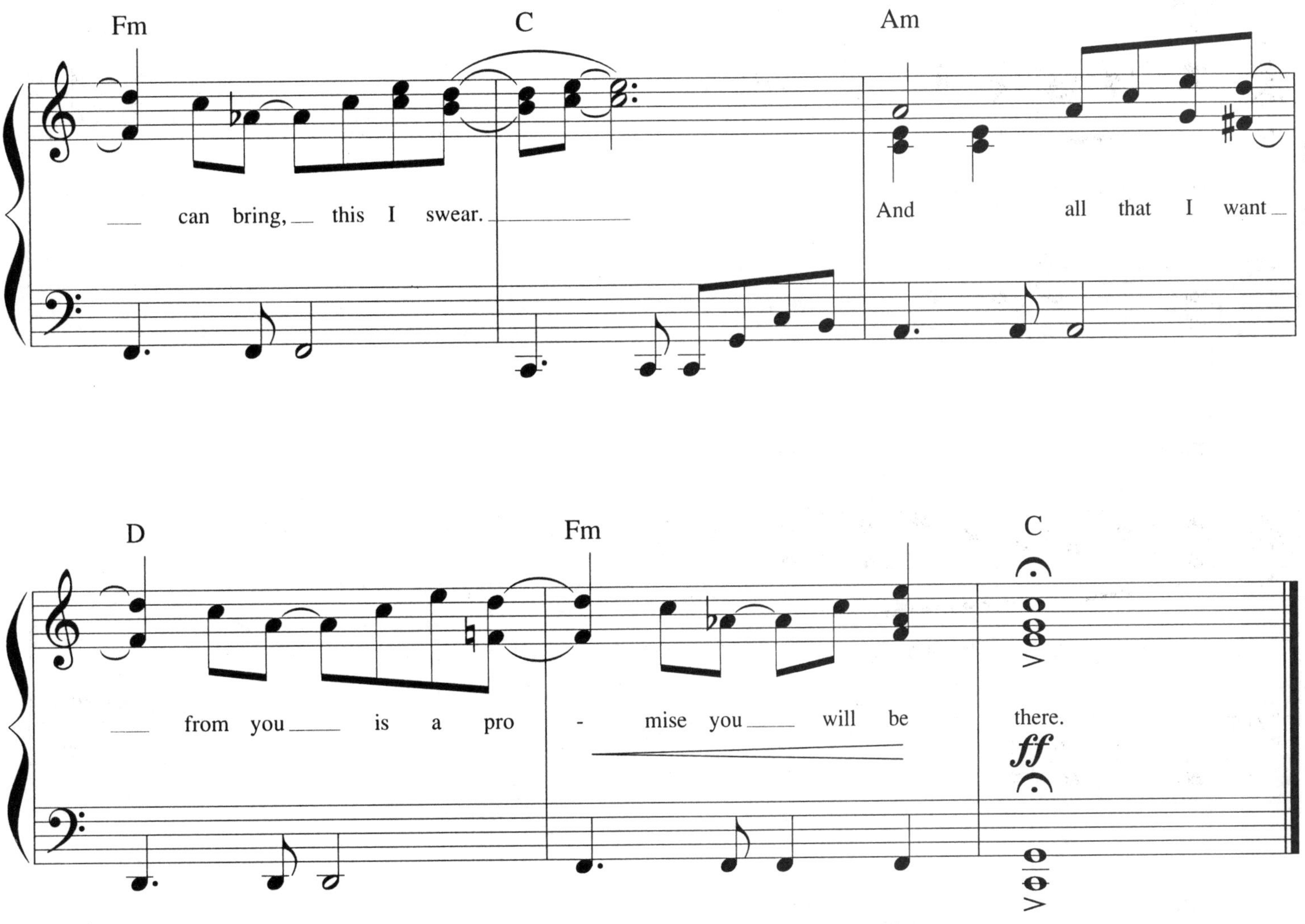

Verse 2:
If you put two and two together,
You will see what our friendship is for.
If you can't work out the equation
Then I guess I'll have to show you the door.
There is no need to say you love me,
It would be better left unsaid.

I'm giving you everything,
All that joy can bring,
This I swear.
And all that I want from you
Is a promise you will be there.

BUTTERFLY KISSES

Words and Music by
BOB CARLISLE and RANDY THOMAS
Arranged by DAN COATES

Dm7 C/E F Gsus4 G F G
she talks to Je - sus, and I close my eyes. And I thank God for all of the
C F F/G
joy in my life. Oh, but most of all, for
cresc.
Chorus:
C
but - ter - fly kiss - es af - ter bed - time prayer, stick - in'
mf
G/C Am G
lit - tle white flow - ers all up in her hair.

F
C
"Walk be - side the po - ny, dad - dy, it's my first ride." "I
F
C
know the cake looks fun - ny, dad - dy, but I sure tried." Oh, with
F
G
C
Dsus4
D
To Coda
all that I've done wrong, I must have done some - thing right to de - serve a
cresc.
F
G7
1.
C
hug ev - 'ry morn - ing and but - ter - fly kiss - es at night.
dim.
mp

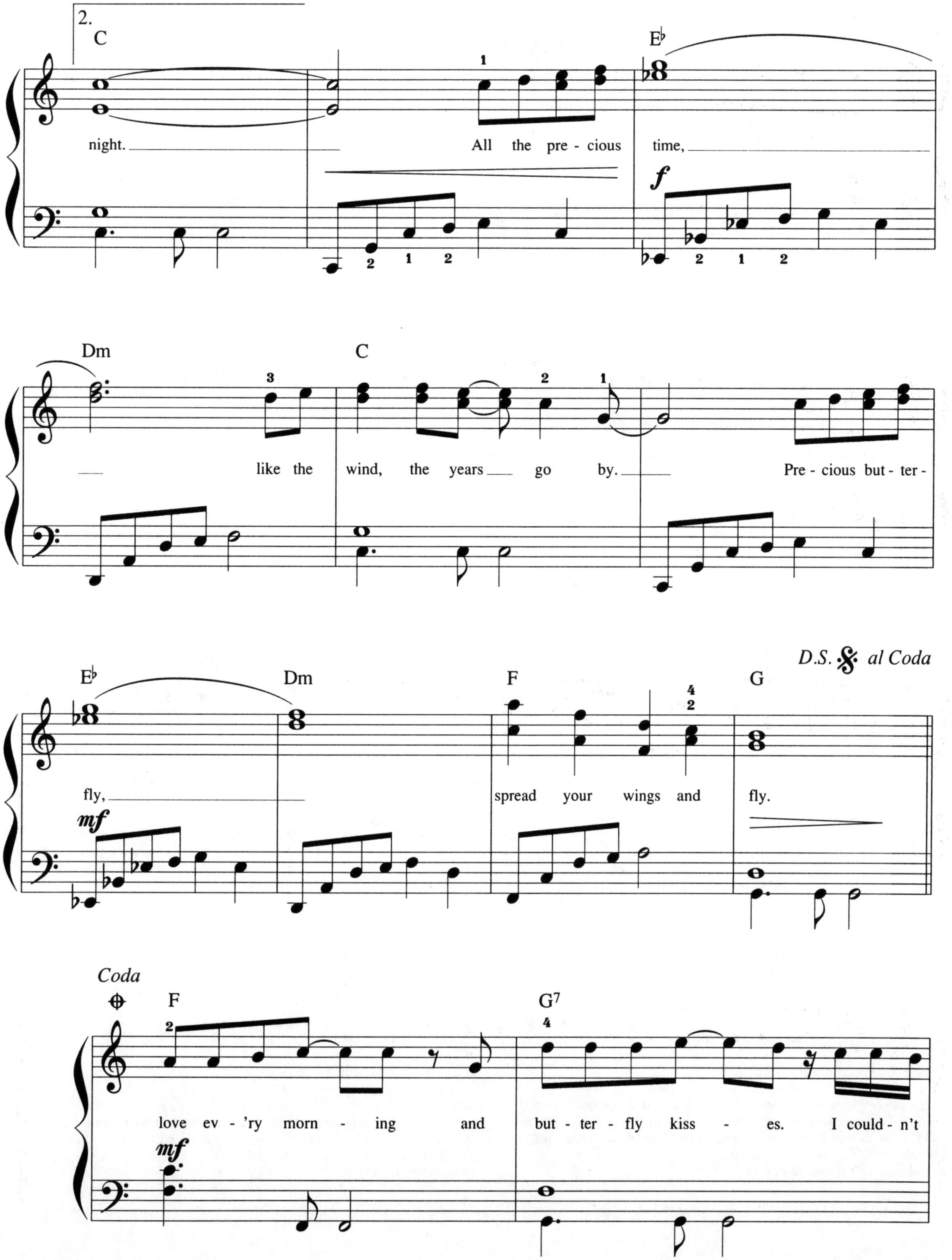
2.
C
E♭
night.
All the pre - cious
time,
f
Dm
C
like the
wind, the years go by.
Pre - cious but - ter -
D.S. 𝄋 al Coda
E♭
Dm
F
G
fly,
spread your wings and
fly.
mf
Coda
F
G7
love ev - 'ry morn - ing and
but - ter - fly kiss - es. I could - n't
mf

Verse 2:
Sweet sixteen today,
She's lookin' like her mama a little more every day.
One part woman, the other part girl;
To perfume and make-up from ribbons and curls.
Trying her wings out in a great big world.
But I remember:

Chorus 2:
Butterfly kisses after bedtime prayer,
Stickin' little white flowers all up in her hair.
"You know how much I love you, daddy, but if you don't mind,
I'm only gonna kiss you on the cheek this time."
Oh, with all that I've done wrong, I must have done something right
To deserve her love every morning
And butterfly kisses at night.

Verse 3:
She'll change her name today.
She'll make a promise, and I'll give her away.
Standing in the brideroom just staring at her,
She asks me what I'm thinking, and I say, "I'm not sure.
I just feel like I'm losing my baby girl."
Then she leaned over and gave me...

Chorus 3:
Butterfly kisses with her mama there,
Stickin' little white flowers all up in her hair.
"Walk me down the aisle, daddy, it's just about time."
"Does my wedding gown look pretty, daddy? Daddy, don't cry."
Oh, with all that I've done wrong, I must have done something right
To deserve her love every morning
And butterfly kisses. *(Coda)*

I DON'T WANT TO

Words and Music by
R. KELLY
Arranged by DAN COATES

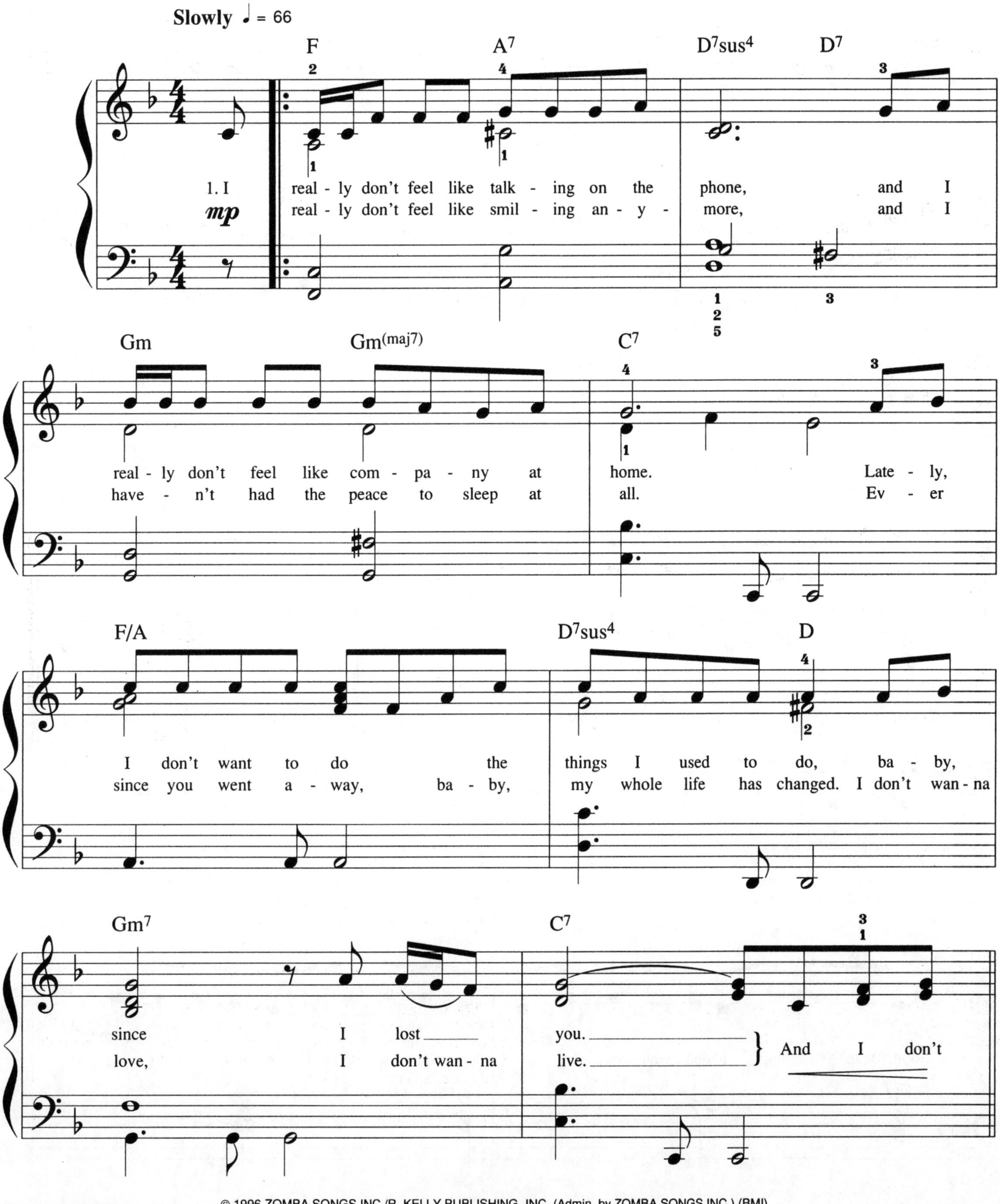

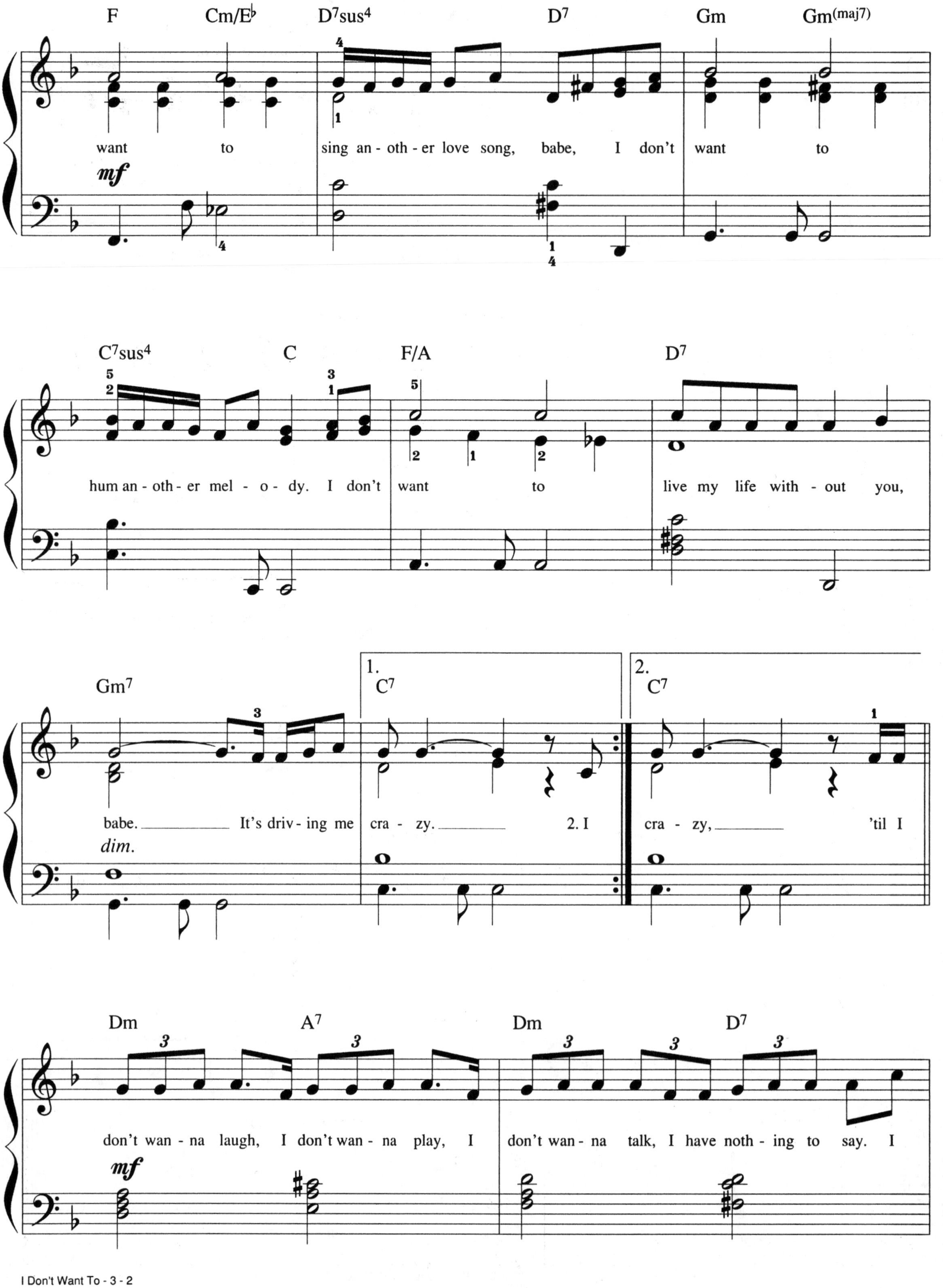
F Cm/E♭ D7sus4 D7 Gm Gm(maj7)
want to sing an - oth - er love song, babe, I don't want to
mf
C7sus4 C F/A D7
hum an - oth - er mel - o - dy. I don't want to live my life with - out you,
Gm7
1. C7
2. C7
babe. It's driv - ing me cra - zy. 2. I cra - zy, 'til I
dim.
Dm A7 Dm D7
don't wan - na laugh, I don't wan - na play, I don't wan - na talk, I have noth - ing to say. I
mf

Gm
C7sus4
C7
D7sus4
D
don't wan - na tour, for - get the show. How can I go on, now that you are gone? I don't
cresc.
G
Dm/F
E7sus4
E7
Am
Am(maj7)
want to sing an - oth - er love song, babe, I don't want to
f
D7sus4
D
G/B
E7
hum an - oth - er mel - o - dy. I don't want to live my life with - out you,
Am7
D7
Cmaj7
Bm7
babe. It's driv - ing me cra - zy. (And I don't)
mf
Am7
C/D
G
C/G
G
mp
rit.

YOU WERE MEANT FOR ME

Words and Music by
JEWEL KILCHER and STEVE POLTZ
Arranged by DAN COATES

C
G/B
C
I break the yolks and make a smil - y face, I kind of like it in my
Em
C
G/B
brand new place. I wipe the spots a - bove the mirror, don't leave the keys in the door. I
C
D
C
nev - er put wet tow - els on the floor an - y - more, 'cause dreams last for
cresc.
mf
D
G
D/F♯
Em
G/D
so long, ev - en af - ter you're gone.

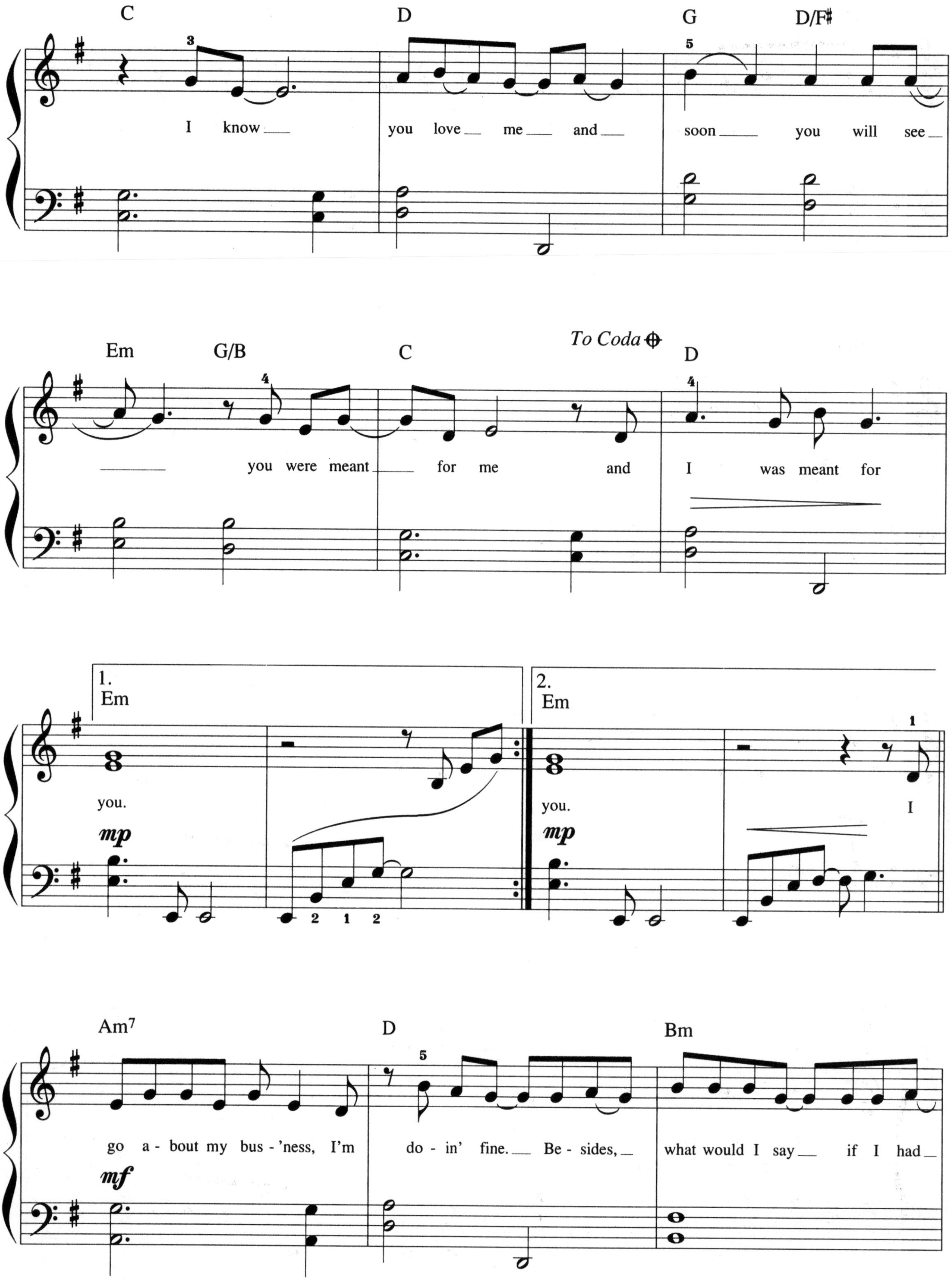
C
D
G
D/F♯
I know
you love me and
soon you will see
Em
G/B
C
To Coda
D
you were meant for me and
I was meant for
1.
Em
you.
mp
2.
Em
you.
mp
I
Am7
D
Bm
go a - bout my bus - 'ness, I'm
do - in' fine. Be - sides,
what would I say if I had
mf

D Em Am7 D
___ you on the line? Same old sto - ry, not much to say.
Bm7 Em C
Hearts are bro - ken ev - 'ry day.___
D.S. al Coda
G/B C Em
dim.
Coda
D Em
I was meant for you. You were

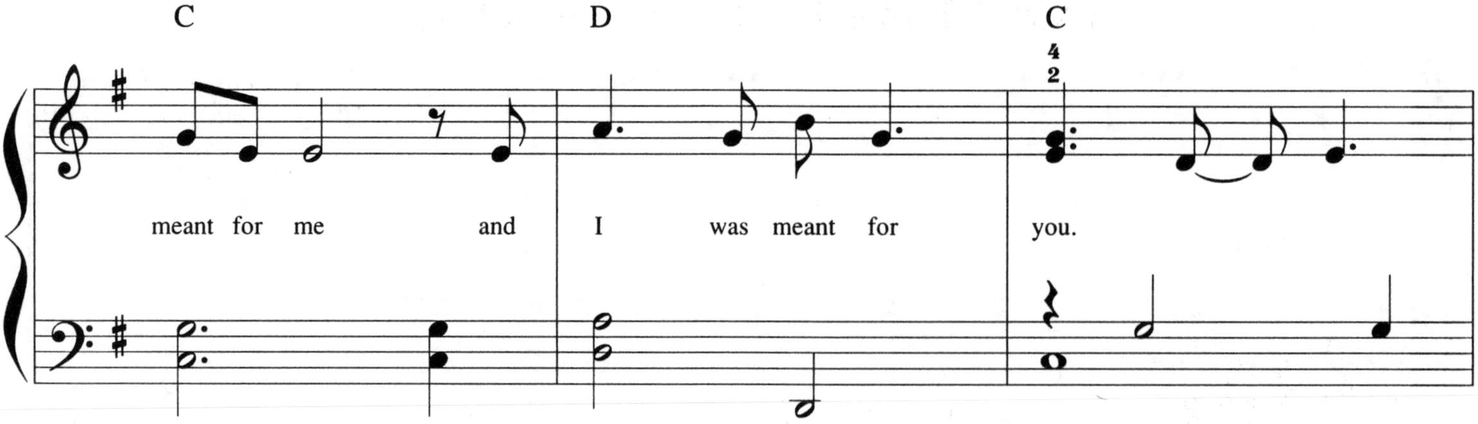

Verse 2:
I called my mama, she was out for a walk.
Consoled a cup of coffee, but it didn't wanna talk.
So I picked up a paper, it was more bad news,
More hearts being broken or people being used.
Put on my coat in the pouring rain.
I saw a movie, it just wasn't the same,
'Cause it was happy and I was sad,
And it made me miss you, oh, so bad.
(To Chorus:)

Verse 3:
I brush my teeth and put the cap back on,
I know you hate it when I leave the light on.
I pick a book up and then I turn the sheets down,
And then I take a breath and a good look around.
Put on my pj's and hop into bed.
I'm half alive but I feel mostly dead.
I try and tell myself it'll be all right,
I just shouldn't think anymore tonight.
(To Chorus:)

TOO LATE, TOO SOON

Words and Music by
JON SECADA, JAMES HARRIS III
and TERRY LEWIS
Arranged by DAN COATES

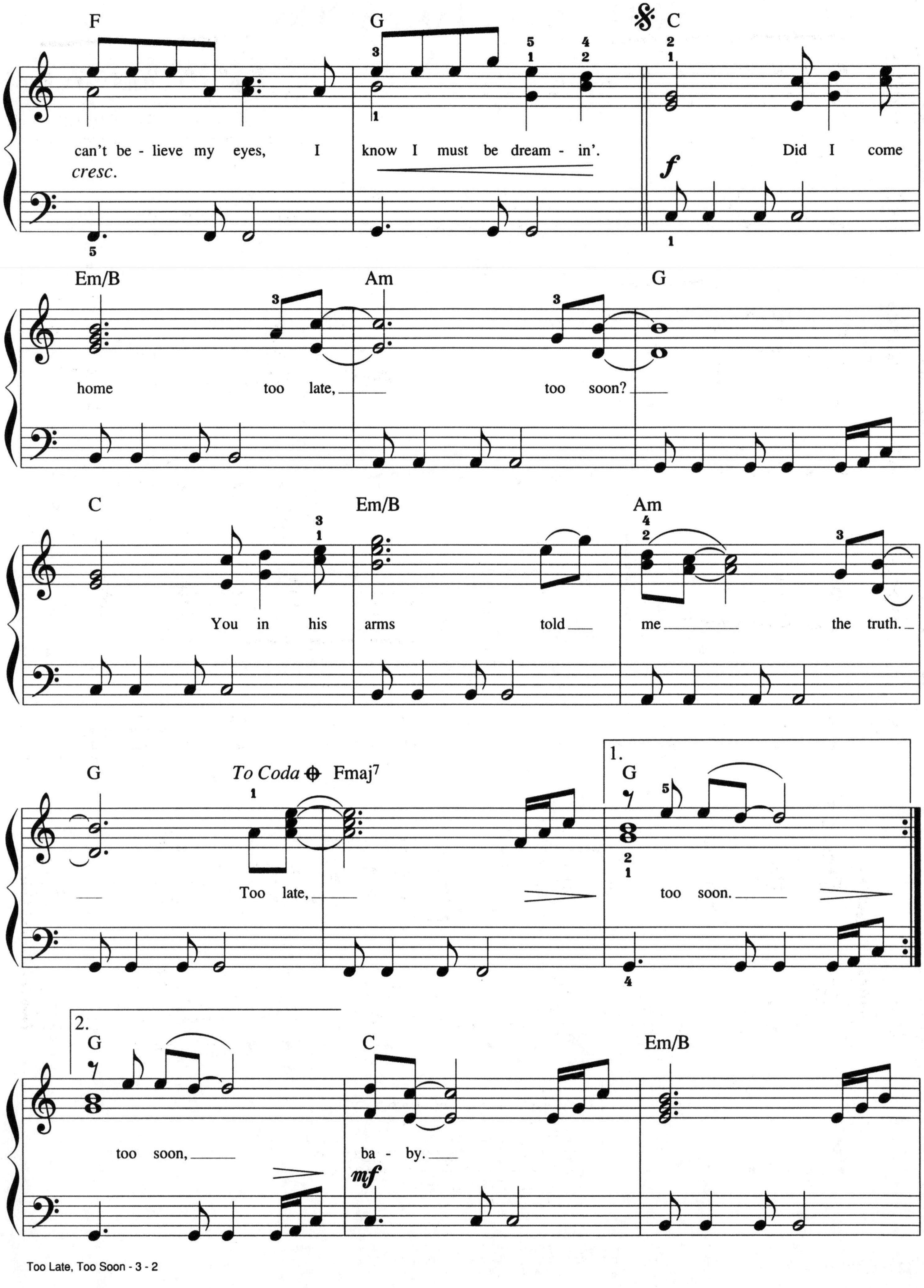
F
G
C
can't be - lieve my eyes, I
know I must be dream - in'.
Did I come
cresc.
f
Em/B
Am
G
home too late,
too soon?
C
Em/B
Am
You in his arms told
me the truth.
G
To Coda
Fmaj7
1.
G
Too late,
too soon.
2.
G
C
Em/B
too soon,
ba - by.
mf

Verse 2:
I wish I would have known,
I wouldn't have left you all alone.
Temptation led you wrong.
Tell me how long this has been goin' on?
'Cause I thought our love was strong,
But I guess I must be dreamin'.
(To Chorus:)

QUIT PLAYING GAMES
(With My Heart)

Words and Music by
MAX MARTIN and HERBERT CRICHLOW
Arranged by DAN COATES

G
Am
be.
see?
Some - times I wish I could
turn back
time,
im -
F
G
pos - si - ble as it may
seem. But I wish I could
so
Am
F
bad,
ba -
by.
cresc.
Quit play - ing games with my
G
Am
F
heart,
with my
heart,
my
heart.
f

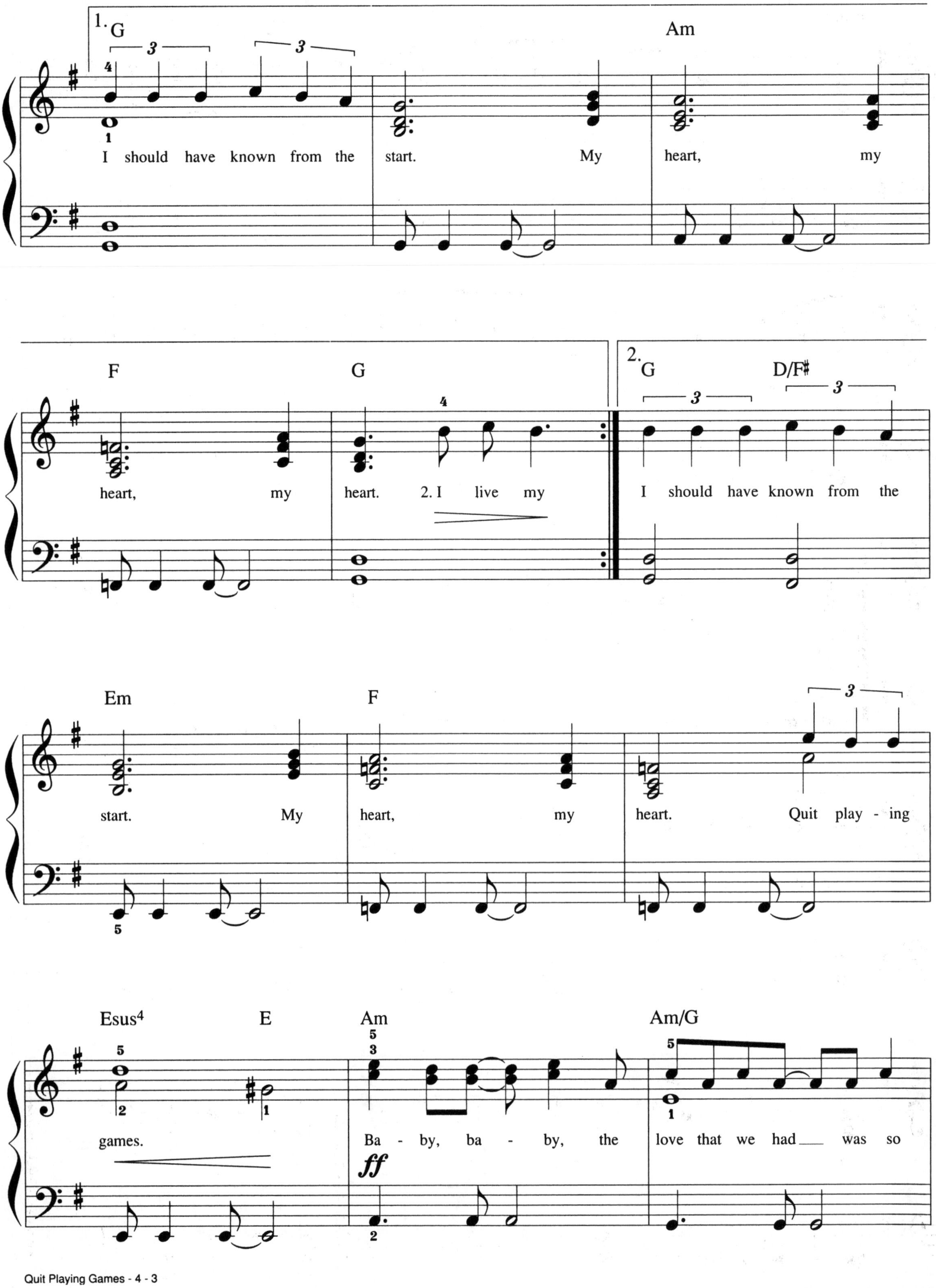
1.
G
Am
I should have known from the start. My heart, my
F
G
2.
G
D/F♯
heart, my heart. 2. I live my
I should have known from the
Em
F
start. My heart, my heart. Quit play - ing
Esus4
E
Am
Am/G
games.
Ba - by, ba - by, the love that we had was so
ff

Fmaj7 F G Am
strong. Don't leave me hang - ing here for - ev - er. Oh, ba - by, ba - by,
Am/G Fmaj7
this is not right. Let's stop this to - night.
Quit play - ing games with my
G Am F
heart, with my heart, my heart.
G D/F# Em F
I should have known from the start. My heart, my
heart.
1. G
Quit play - ing games with my
2.
Quit play - ing games!

FOR YOU I WILL

Words and Music by
DIANE WARREN
Arranged by DAN COATES

Moderately slow ♩ = 72

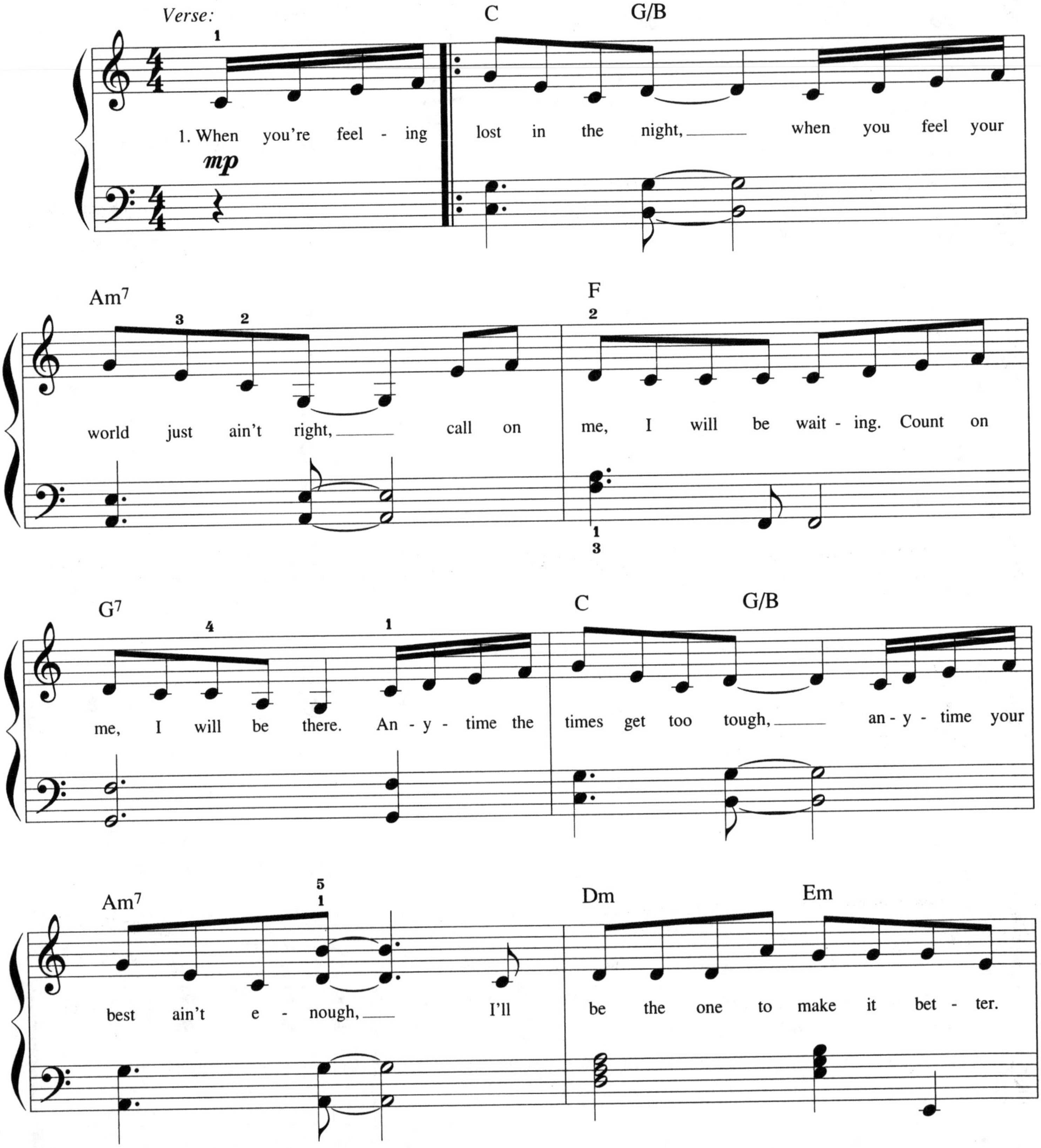

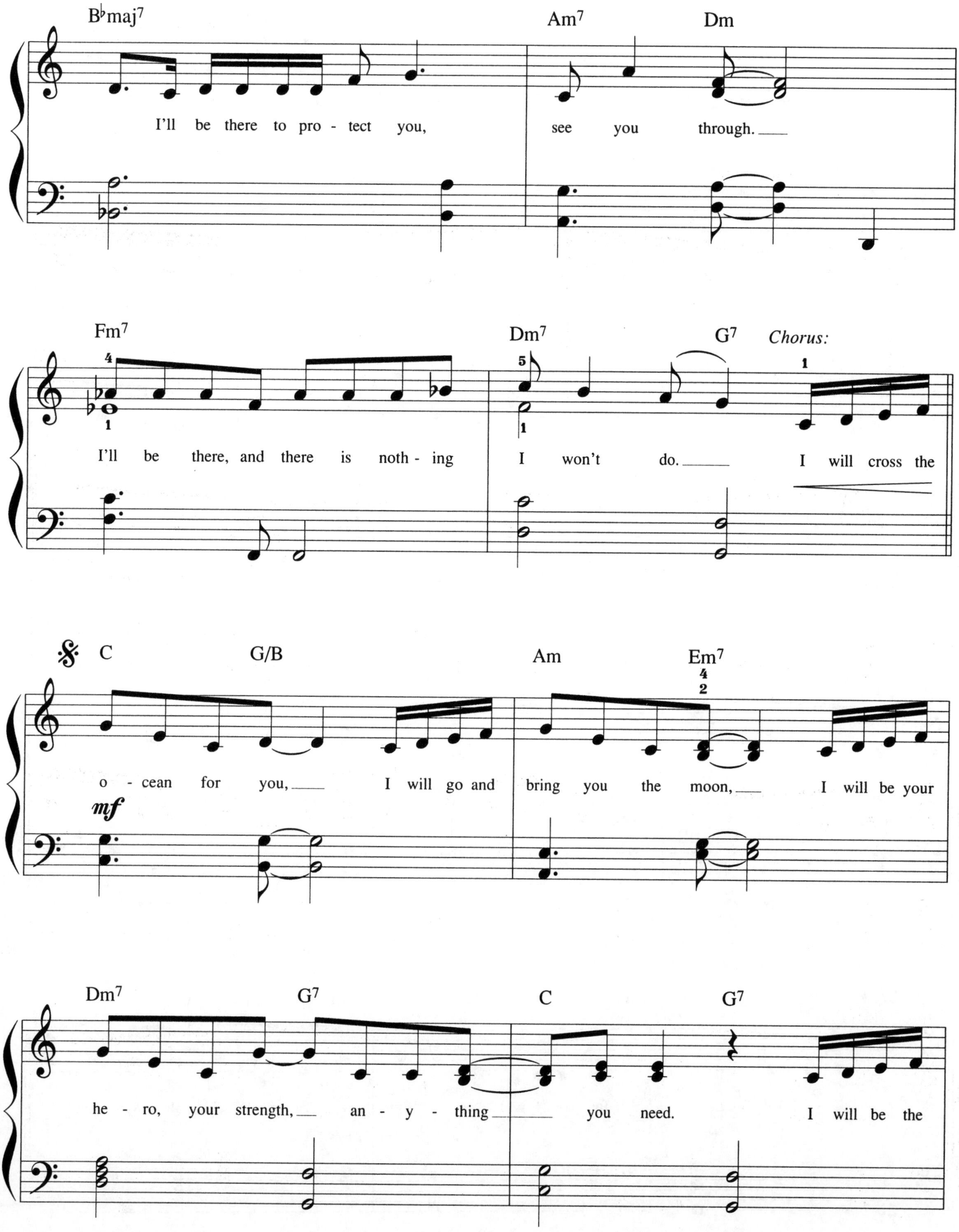
B♭maj7
I'll be there to pro - tect you,
Am7 Dm
see you through.
Fm7
I'll be there, and there is noth - ing
Dm7 G7
I won't do.
Chorus:
I will cross the
C G/B
o - cean for you,
I will go and
mf
Am Em7
bring you the moon,
I will be your
Dm7 G7
he - ro, your strength,
an - y - thing
C G7
you need.
I will be the

C G/B Am7 Em7
sun in your sky, I will light your way for all time, prom - ise
To Coda
1.
Dm G7 C G7sus4 G7
you, for you I will. 2. I will shield your
mp
2.
C B♭ F/A C
will. For you, I will lay my life on the line.
mp
mf
E/G♯ Am7 Dm C/E
For you, I'll fight, for you, I will die. With ev - 'ry breath, with all my soul, I
cresc.

D.S. 𝄋 al Coda
E7 Am Fm7 G7
give my word, I'll give it all. Put your faith in me, I'll do an - y - thing. I will cross the
f
C Dm G7
Coda
will. Prom - ise you, for you I
mp
C Dm G7 C
will. I prom - ise you, for you I will.
rit. e dim.
p

Verse 2:
I will shield your heart from the rain,
I won't let no harm come your way.
Oh, these arms will be your shelter,
No, these arms won't let you down.
If there is a mountain to move,
I will move that mountain for you.
I'm here for you, I'm here forever.
I will be a fortress, tall and strong.
I'll keep you safe, I'll stand beside you,
Right or wrong. *(To Chorus:)*

I BELIEVE I CAN FLY

Words and Music by
R. KELLY
Arranged by DAN COATES

Am7
Fm/A♭
see it, then I can do it, if I just be -
mf
C/G
G7
lieve it, there's noth - ing to it. I be - lieve I can
C
Am7
fly, I be - lieve I can touch the sky. I think a - bout it ev - 'ry
f
Dm7
G7
G♯dim7
night and day, spread my wings and fly a - way. I be - lieve I can

Am7
Dm7(♭5)
soar, I see me run - ning through that
o - pen door. I be - lieve I can
C/G
Fm/G
To Coda
fly, I be - lieve I can
dim.
fly, I be - lieve I can
mf
1.
Am
F/G
fly.
See,
mp
2.
Am
fly.
mp
Dm7
C/E
F
E7
Hey, 'cause I be - lieve in
me.
If I can

Am7
Fm/A♭
see it, then I can do it, if I just be -
mf
D.S. 𝄋 al Coda
C/G
G7
lieve it, there's noth - ing to it. I be - lieve I can
Coda
C/G
Fm/A♭
C/G
fly. If I just spread my wings, I can fly. If I just
mp
Fm/G
C
Fm/A♭
C
spread my wings, I can fly.
rit. e dim.
p

From the Motion Picture "THE MIRROR HAS TWO FACES"

I FINALLY FOUND SOMEONE

Written by
BARBRA STREISAND, MARVIN HAMLISCH,
R. J. LANGE and BRYAN ADAMS
Arranged by DAN COATES

B♭
Gm7
It start - ed o - ver cof - fee,
we start - ed out as friends.
E♭maj7
Cm7/F
F7
It's fun - ny how from sim - ple things,
the best things be - gin.
cresc.
G
Em7
This time it's dif - f'rent,
it's all be - cause of you.
mf
Cmaj7
Cm6
It's bet - ter than it's ev - er been
'cause we can talk it through.
G
Em7
My fa - v'rite line
was, "Can I call you some - time?"
mp

Cmaj7
Cm
It's all you had to say to take my breathe a - way.
E
This is it! Oh, I fi - n'lly
mf
Amaj7
Am
E
found some - one, some - one to share my life. I fi - n'lly
f
Amaj7
Am
E
found the one to be with ev - 'ry night. 'Cause what -

G#7sus4
G#7
C#m
C
ev - er you do, it's just got to be you. My
E/B
A/B
To Coda
life has just be - gun, I fi - n'lly found some -
decresc.
Emaj7
C#m7
one.
mp
Amaj7
C/D
D

Gmaj7
Did I keep you wait - ing?
mf
Em7
I a - pol - o - gize.
Cmaj7
I will wait for - ev - er just to
Cm
know you were mine.
You know,
G
I love your hair,
I
Em
love what you wear.
C
Well, you're ex - cep - tion - al! I can't
Cm
wait for the rest of my life!
D.S. al Coda
E
This is it!
Oh,
I fi - n'lly
cresc.

Coda
B/C♯
C♯7
F♯m
one. And what - ev - er I do, it's just
f
E/G♯
A/B
got to be you. Oh, my life has just be - gun,
dim.
E
I fi - n'lly found some -
mp
A
Emaj7
8va
one.
rit. e dim.
p

I LOVE YOU ALWAYS FOREVER

Words and Music by
DONNA LEWIS
Arranged by DAN COATES

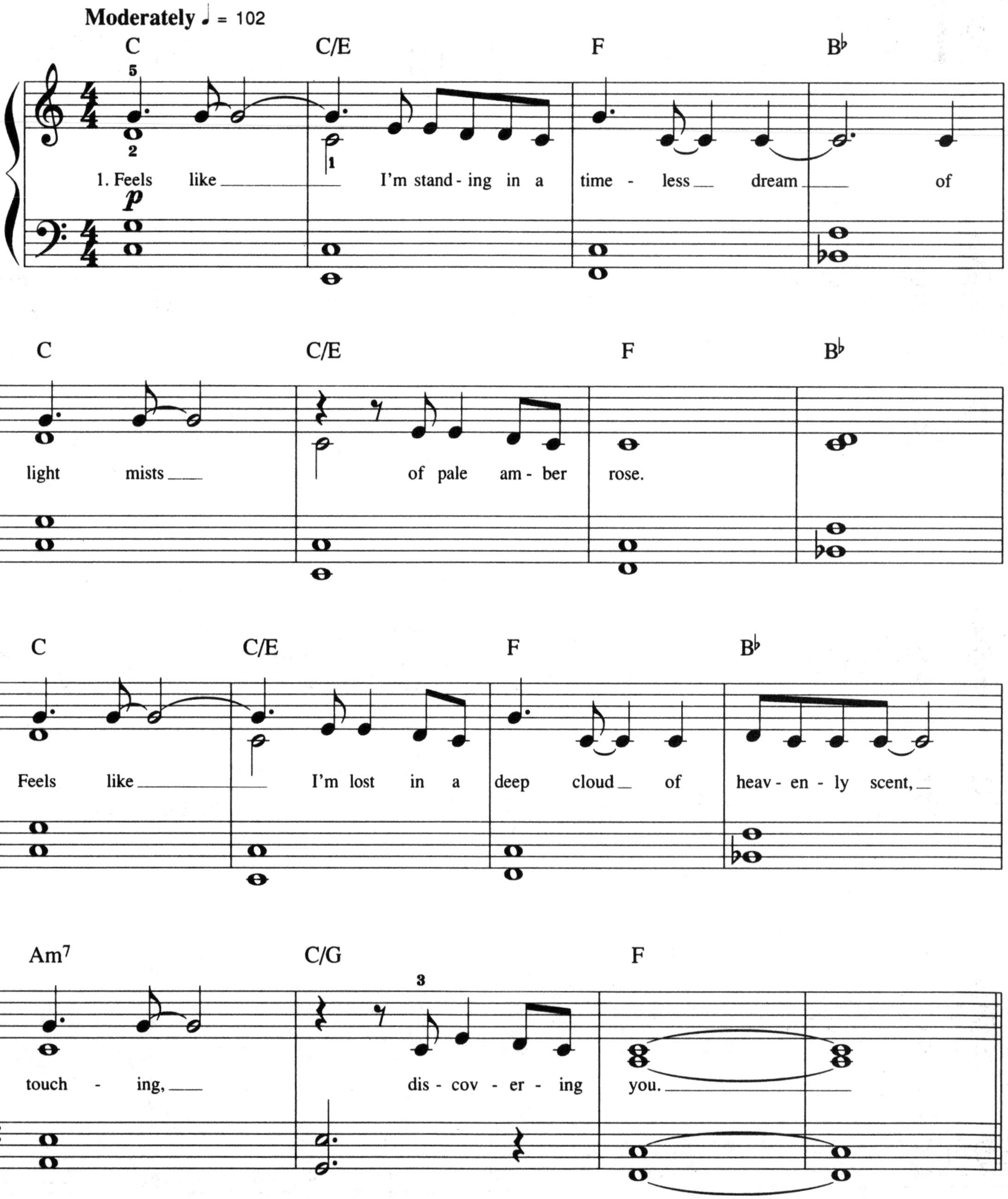

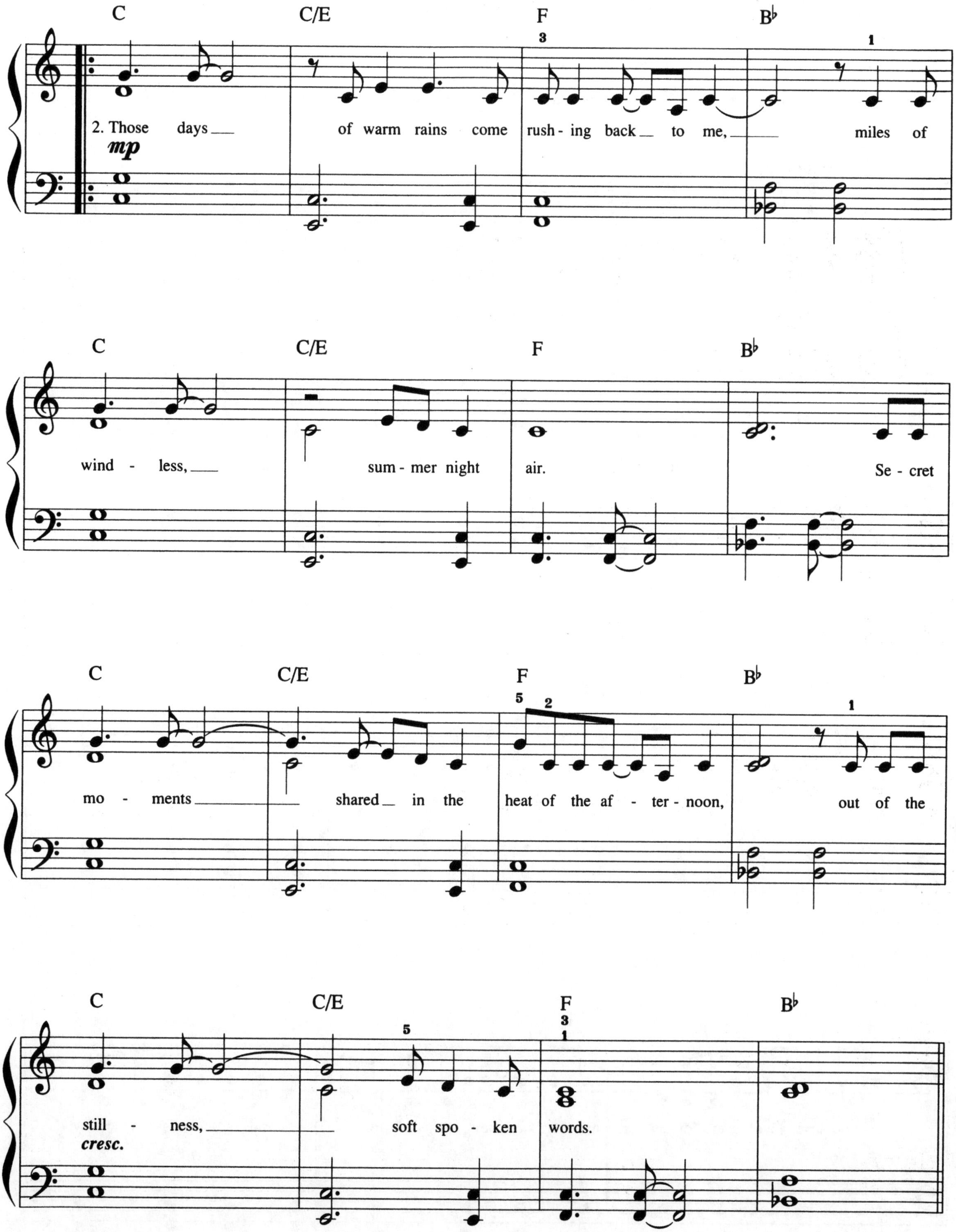
C
C/E
F
B♭
3
1
2. Those days __ of warm rains come rush - ing back __ to me, __ miles of
mp
C
C/E
F
B♭
wind - less, __ sum - mer night air. Se - cret
C
C/E
F
B♭
5
2
1
mo - ments __ shared __ in the heat of the af - ter - noon, out of the
C
C/E
F
B♭
5
3
1
still - ness, __ soft spo - ken words.
cresc.

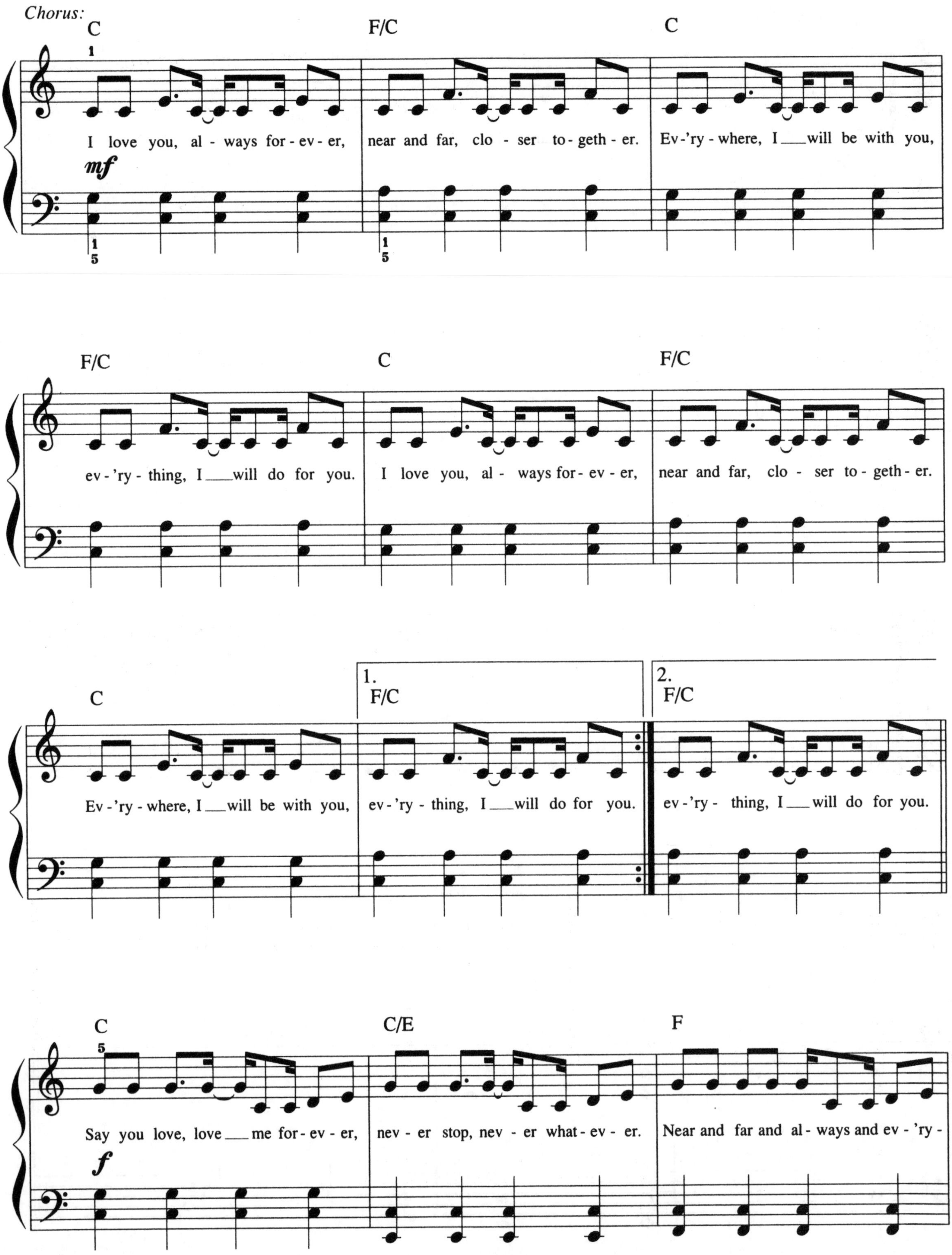
Chorus:
C
F/C
C
I love you, al - ways for - ev - er,
near and far, clo - ser to - geth - er.
Ev - 'ry - where, I ___ will be with you,
mf
F/C
C
F/C
ev - 'ry - thing, I ___ will do for you.
I love you, al - ways for - ev - er,
near and far, clo - ser to - geth - er.
C
1.
F/C
2.
F/C
Ev - 'ry - where, I ___ will be with you,
ev - 'ry - thing, I ___ will do for you.
ev - 'ry - thing, I ___ will do for you.
C
C/E
F
Say you love, love ___ me for - ev - er,
nev - er stop, nev - er what - ev - er.
Near and far and al - ways and ev - 'ry -
f

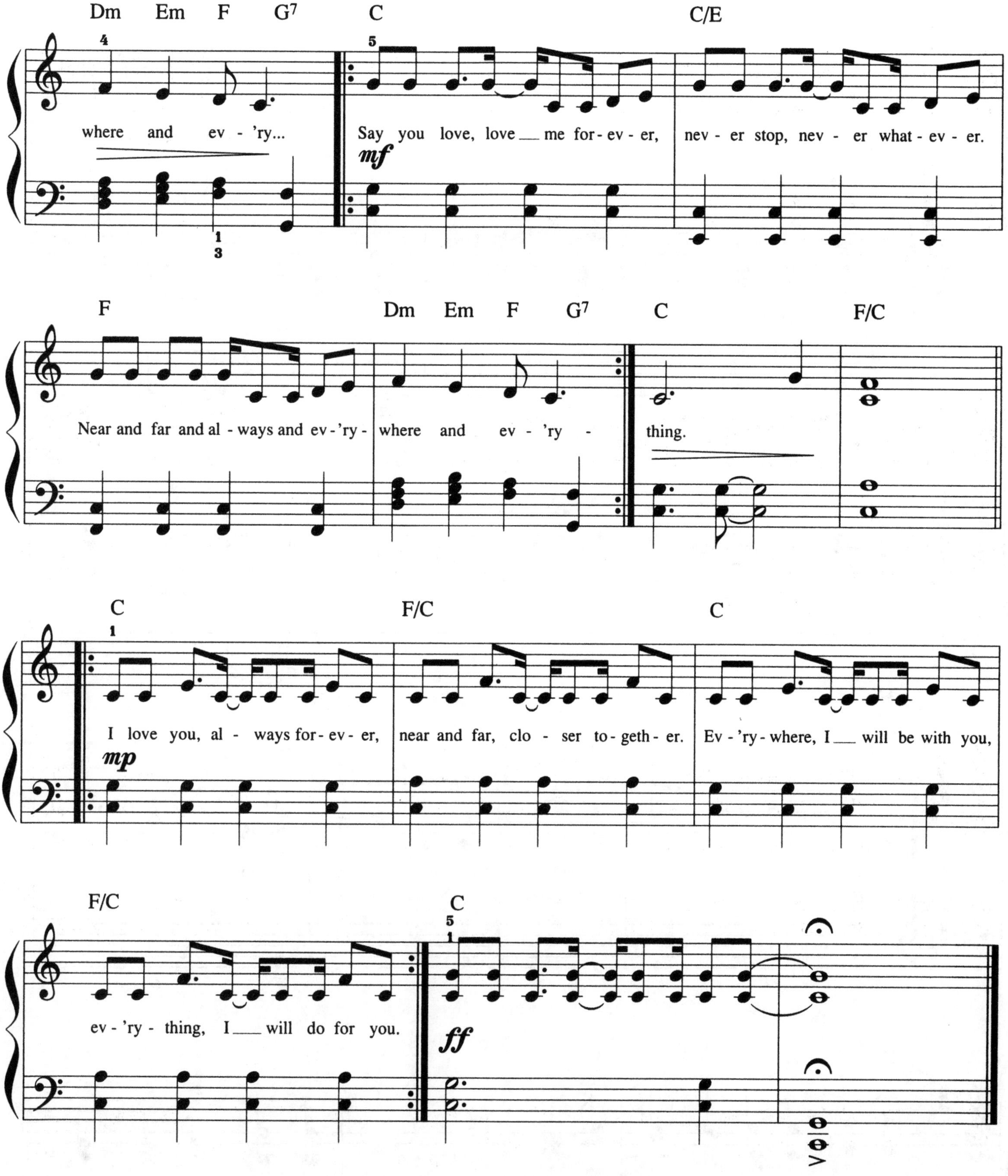

Verse 3:
You've got the most unbelievable blue eyes I've ever seen.
You've got me almost melting away as we lay there
Under blue sky with pure white stars,
Exotic sweetness, a magical time.
(To Chorus:)

BREAKFAST AT TIFFANY'S

Words and Music by
TODD PIPES
Arranged by DAN COATES

Steady rock beat ♩ = 108

D G A
part. You'll say
D G A D
the world has come be - tween us, our
G A D G A
lives have come be - tween us, still I know you just don't
D G A
Chorus:
care. And I
cresc.

D A G D
said what a - bout Break - fast at Tif - fa - ny's, she said I think I re -
A G D A G
mem - ber the film and as I re - call I think we both kind of liked it, and
D 1. A G D
I said well, that's the one thing we got.
G A D G A
2. I

Verse 2:
I see you, the only one who knew me,
But now your eyes see through me.
I guess I was wrong.
So what now?
It's plain to see we're over,
I hate when things are over,
When so much is left undone. *(To Chorus:)*

Verse 3:
You'll say we got nothing in common,
No common ground to start from,
And we're falling apart.
You'll say
The world has come between us,
Our lives have come between us,
Still I know you just don't care. *(To Chorus:)*

BY HEART

Composed by
JIM BRICKMAN and
HOLLYE LEVEN
Arranged by DAN COATES

G7sus4 G F G C
here.
ry.
Un - til the stars fall from the sky, un - til I
mf
F G C B♭
find a rea - son why, and dar - ling as the years go
G F G C
by, un - til there's no tears left to cry, un - til the
F G Am Dm7 C/E
an - gel's close my eyes and ev - en if we're world's a -

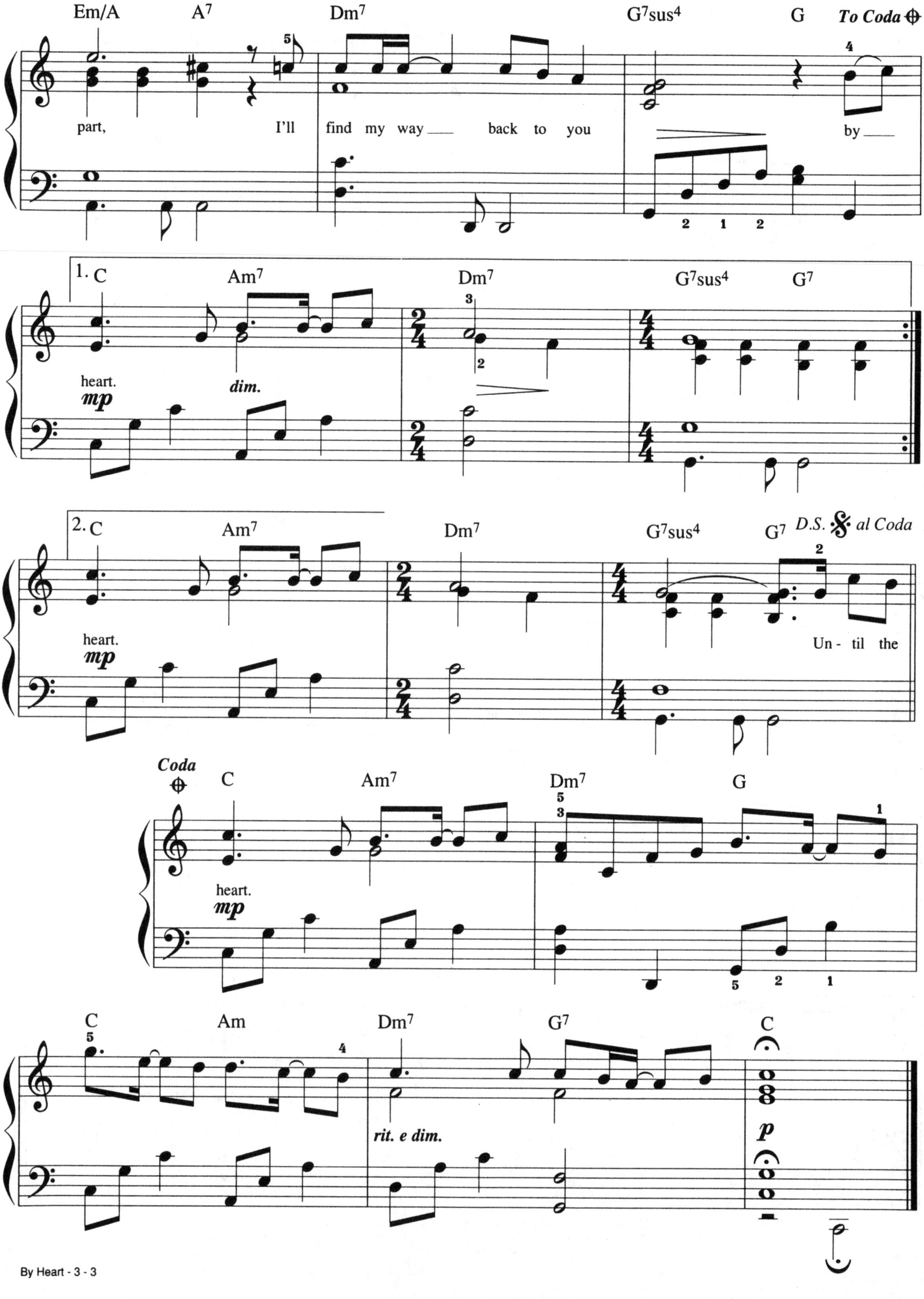
Em/A A7 Dm7 G7sus4 G
To Coda
part, I'll find my way back to you by
1. C Am7 Dm7 G7sus4 G7
heart.
mp
dim.
2. C Am7 Dm7 G7sus4 G7
D.S. al Coda
heart.
mp
Un - til the
Coda
C Am7 Dm7 G
heart.
mp
C Am Dm7 G7 C
rit. e dim.
p

COUNT ON ME

Words and Music by
BABYFACE, WHITNEY HOUSTON
and MICHAEL HOUSTON
Arranged by DAN COATES

D Em7 D/F# Em
I can see it's hurt - ing you. I can feel your pain. It's
mf
D Em7 Am7 D7
hard to see the sun - shine through the rain. I
Gmaj7 A/G F#m7 Bm7
know some - times it seems as if it's nev - er gon - na end, but
Em7 Em7/A
you'll get through it, just don't give in. 'Cause you can
cresc.

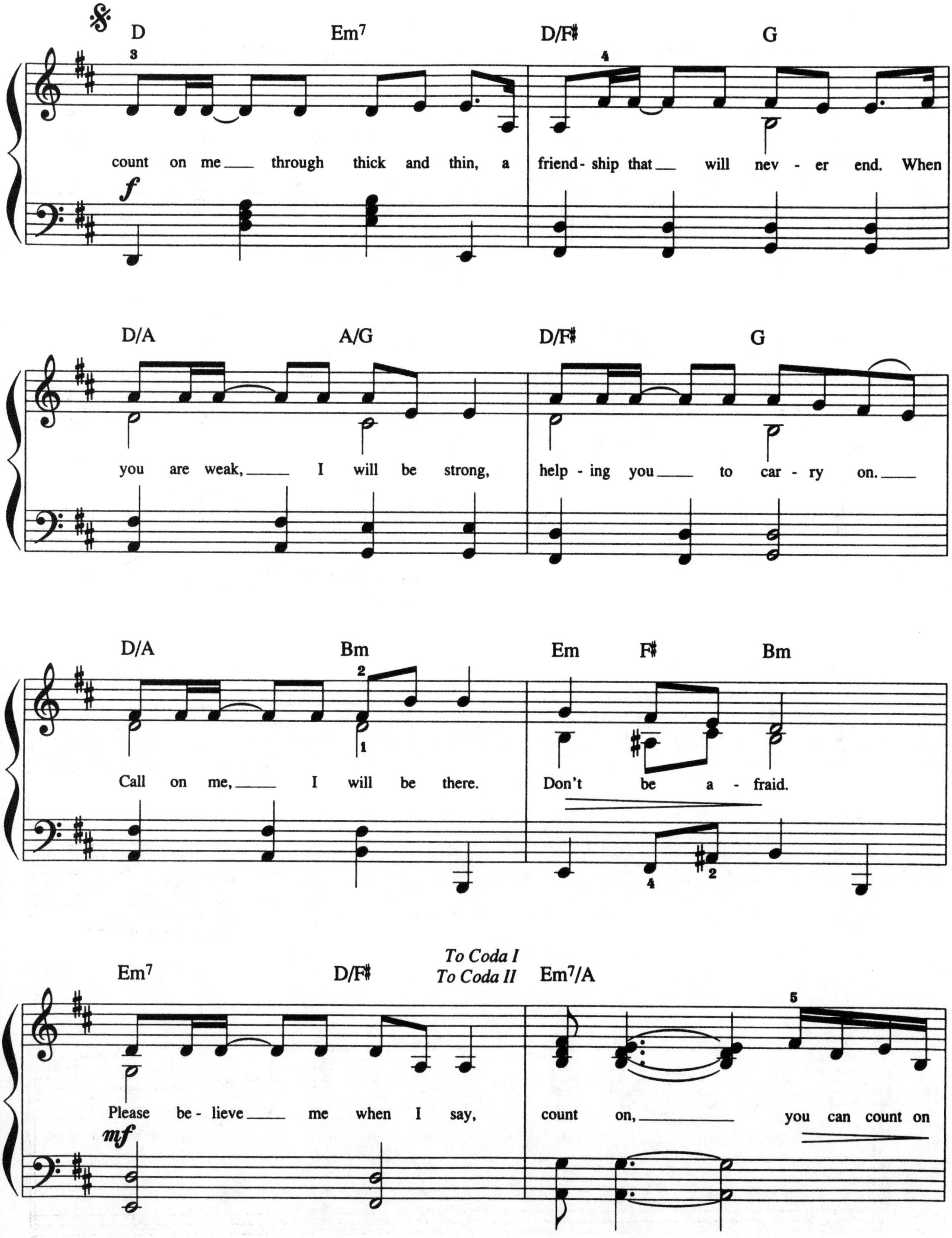
D Em7 D/F♯ G
count on me through thick and thin, a friend-ship that will nev - er end. When
f
D/A A/G D/F♯ G
you are weak, I will be strong, help - ing you to car - ry on.
D/A Bm Em F♯ Bm
Call on me, I will be there. Don't be a - fraid.
To Coda I
To Coda II
Em7 D/F♯ Em7/A
Please be - lieve me when I say, count on, you can count on
mf

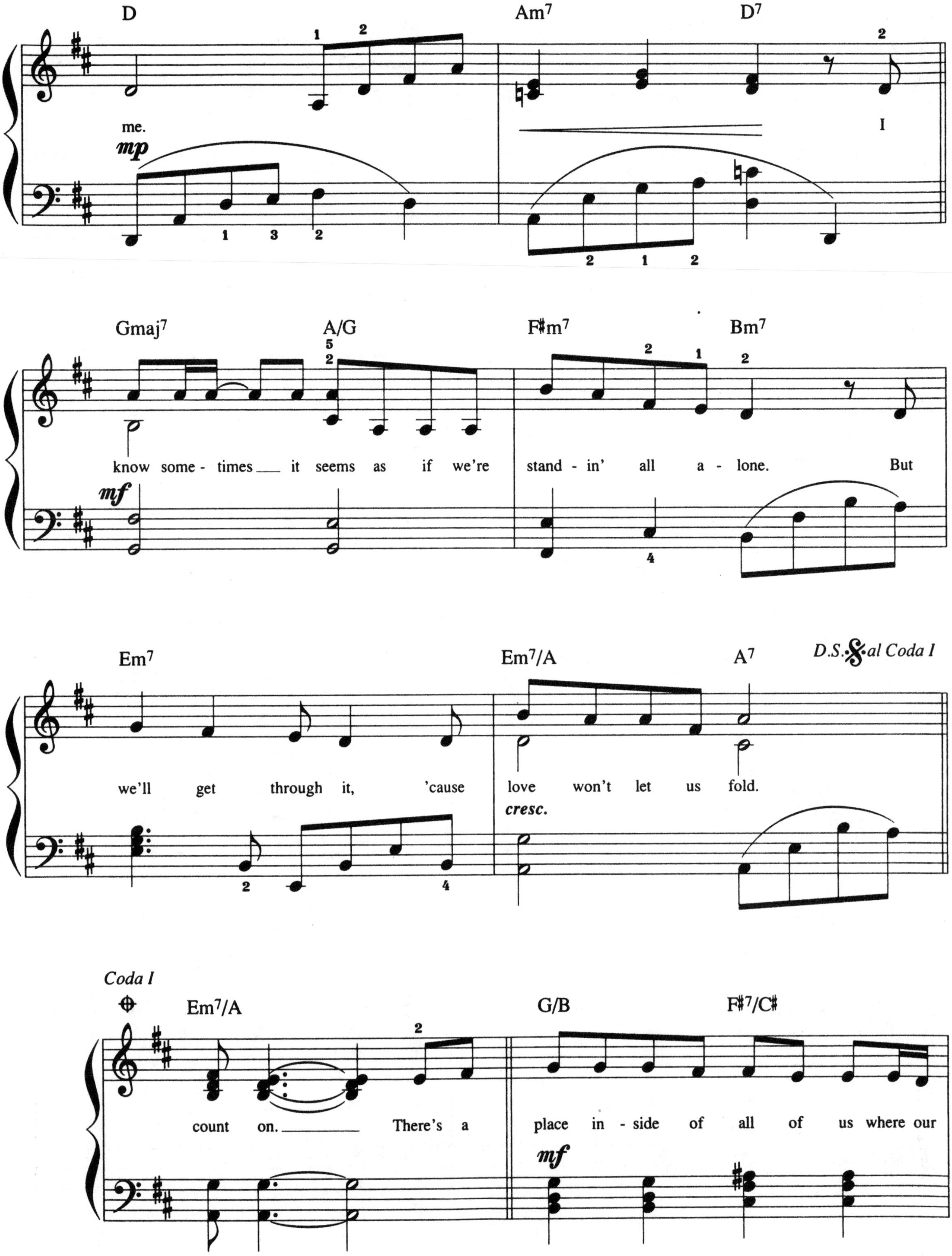
D
1 2
me.
mp
1 3 2
Am7
D7
2
I
2 1 2
Gmaj7
A/G
5
2
F♯m7
2 1
Bm7
2
know some - times ___ it seems as if we're
stand - in' all a - lone. But
mf
4
Em7
Em7/A
A7
D.S. 𝄋 al Coda I
we'll get through it, 'cause
love won't let us fold.
cresc.
2 4
Coda I
𝄌
Em7/A
2
G/B
F♯7/C♯
count on. ________ There's a
place in - side of all of us where our
mf

Bm/D B7/D♯ Em F♯7
faith in love be - gins. You should reach to find the truth in love, the
cresc.
Bm Em A A/G
an - swer's there with - in. I know that life can make you feel it's much
f
D.S. 𝄋 al Coda II
F♯m7 Bm Em7 Em7/A A7
hard - er than it real - ly is, but we'll get through it, just don't, don't give in.
Coda II
Em7/A D Em
count on, count on me, me,
mp
D/F♯ Em G/A D
me, you can count on me.
rit. e dim.
p

FOR YOU

Words and Music by
KENNY LERUM
Arranged by DAN COATES

B♭7
E♭
show my love, or all the thoughts I'm thinking - ing of. 'Cause this
Cm
E♭
A♭maj7
D7sus4
D7
life is no good a - lone, since we've be - come one, I've made a
mf
Gm
Cm
E♭
A♭maj7
Gm
change. And ev - 'ry - thing I do now makes sense, all roads end.
To Coda
1.
Fm
A♭/B♭
E♭
All I do is for you.
2. For
mp

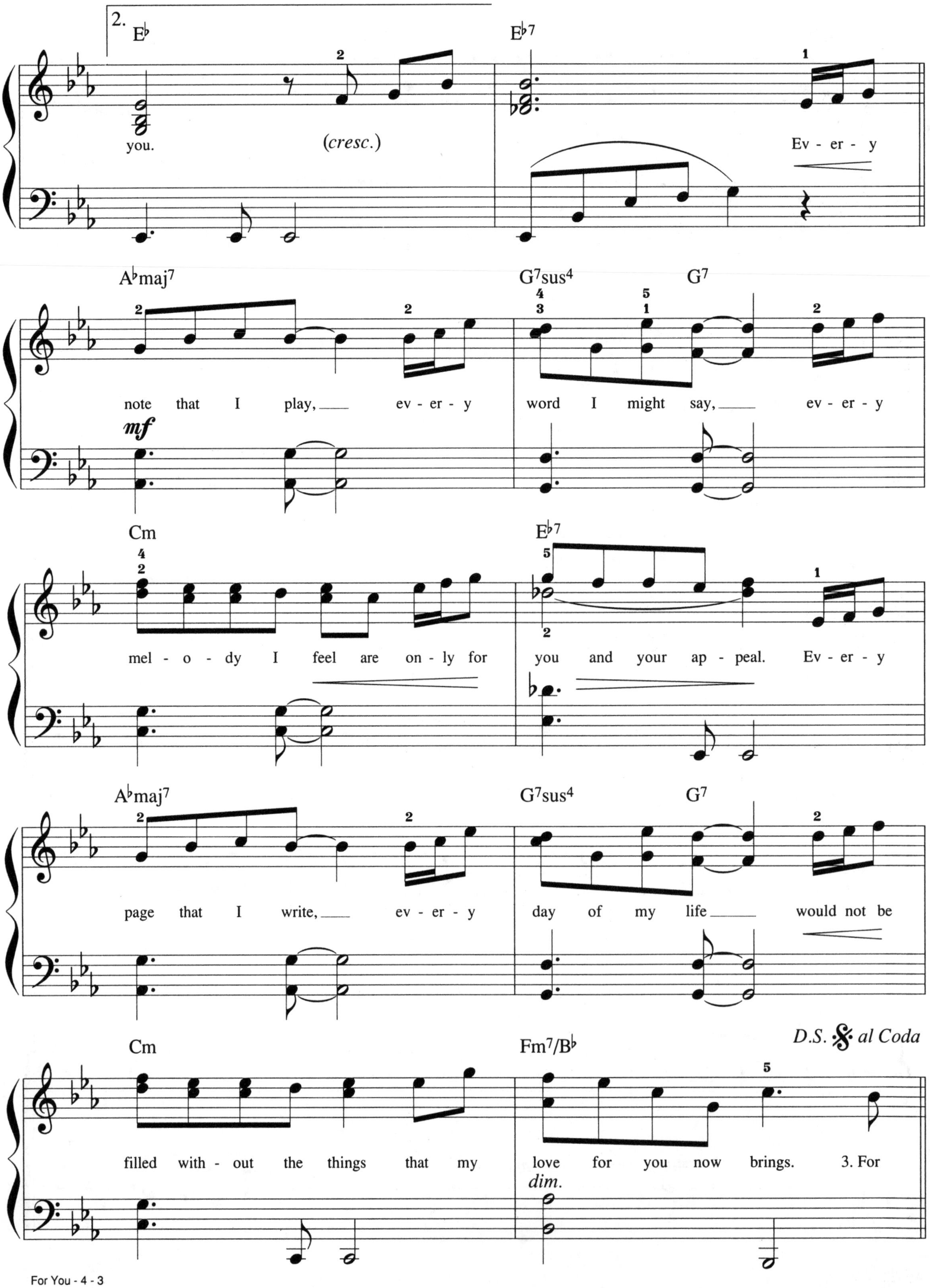
2.
E♭
E♭7
you. (cresc.)
Ev - er - y
A♭maj7
G7sus4
G7
note that I play, ev - er - y word I might say, ev - er - y
mf
Cm
E♭7
mel - o - dy I feel are on - ly for you and your ap - peal. Ev - er - y
A♭maj7
G7sus4
G7
page that I write, ev - er - y day of my life would not be
Cm
Fm7/B♭
D.S. 𝄋 al Coda
filled with - out the things that my love for you now brings. 3. For
dim.

Verse 2:
For you, I share the cup of love that overflows,
And anyone who knows us knows
That I would change all thoughts I have for you.
There is no low or high or in-between
Of my heart that you haven't seen.
'Cause I share all I have and am.
Nothing I've said is hard to understand.
All I feel, I feel deeper still and always will.
All this love is for you.

Verse 3:
For you, I make a promise of fidelity,
Now and for eternity.
No one could replace this love for you,
I take your hand and heart and everything,
And add to them a wedding ring.
'Cause this life is no good alone,
Since we've become one, you're all I know.
If this feeling should leave, I'd die.
And here is why, all I am is for you.

HERO'S DREAM

Composed by
JIM BRICKMAN
Arranged by DAN COATES

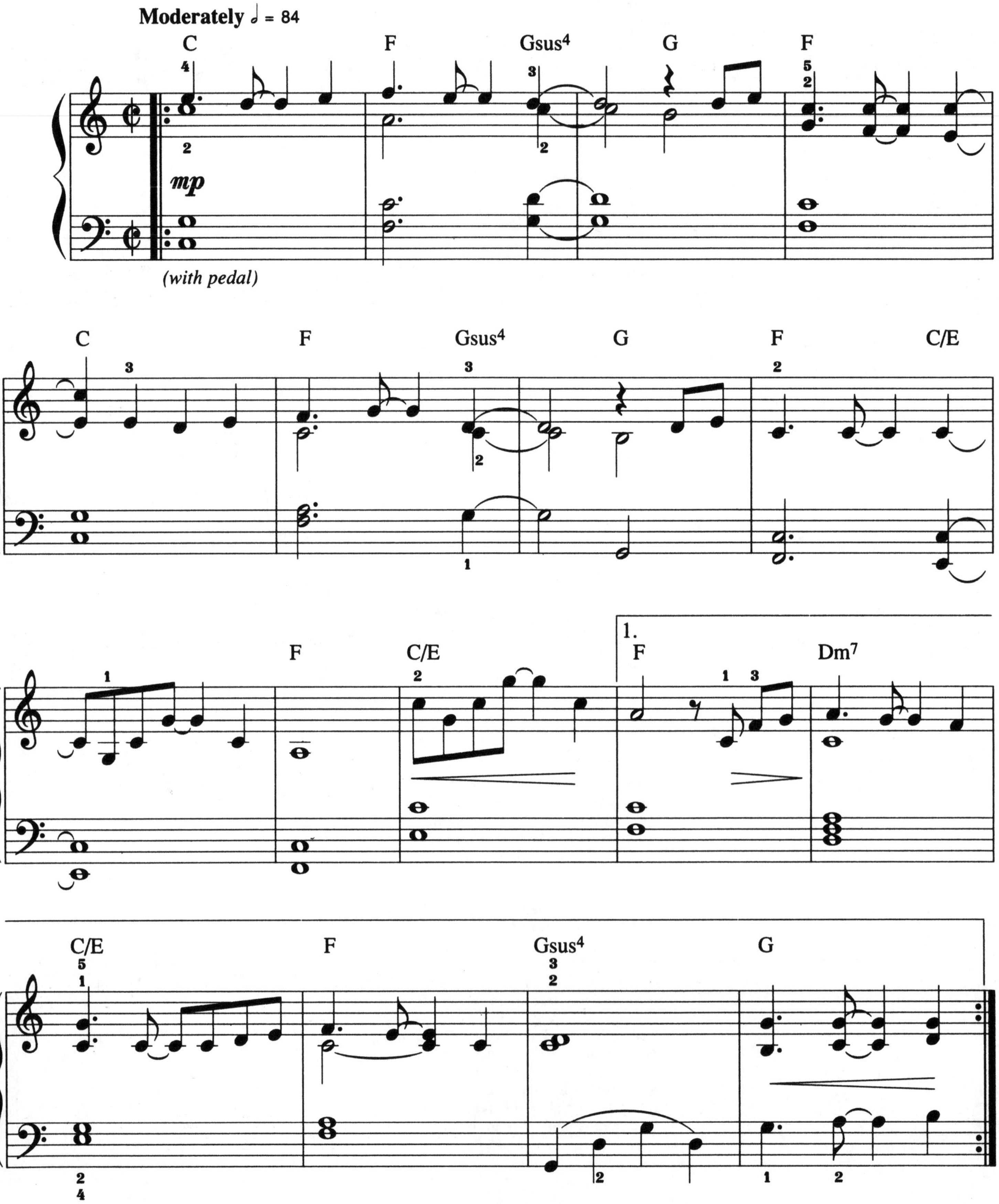

2.
F
Dm7
C/E
F
cresc. poco a poco
Gsus4
G
Am
D/F♯
mf
G
C/E
F
Dm
B♭
G
Am

D/F♯
G
C/E
F
mp cresc.
D/F♯
G
E/G♯
A
mf cresc.
D
G
Asus4
f
A
G
D
G

A
G
D/F♯
G
mf
D/F♯
G
Em
mp
D/F♯
G
D/F♯
cresc. poco a poco
mf
G
A7
G
D
f
rit.

HARD TO SAY I'M SORRY

Words and Music by
DAVID FOSTER and PETER CETERA
Arranged by DAN COATES

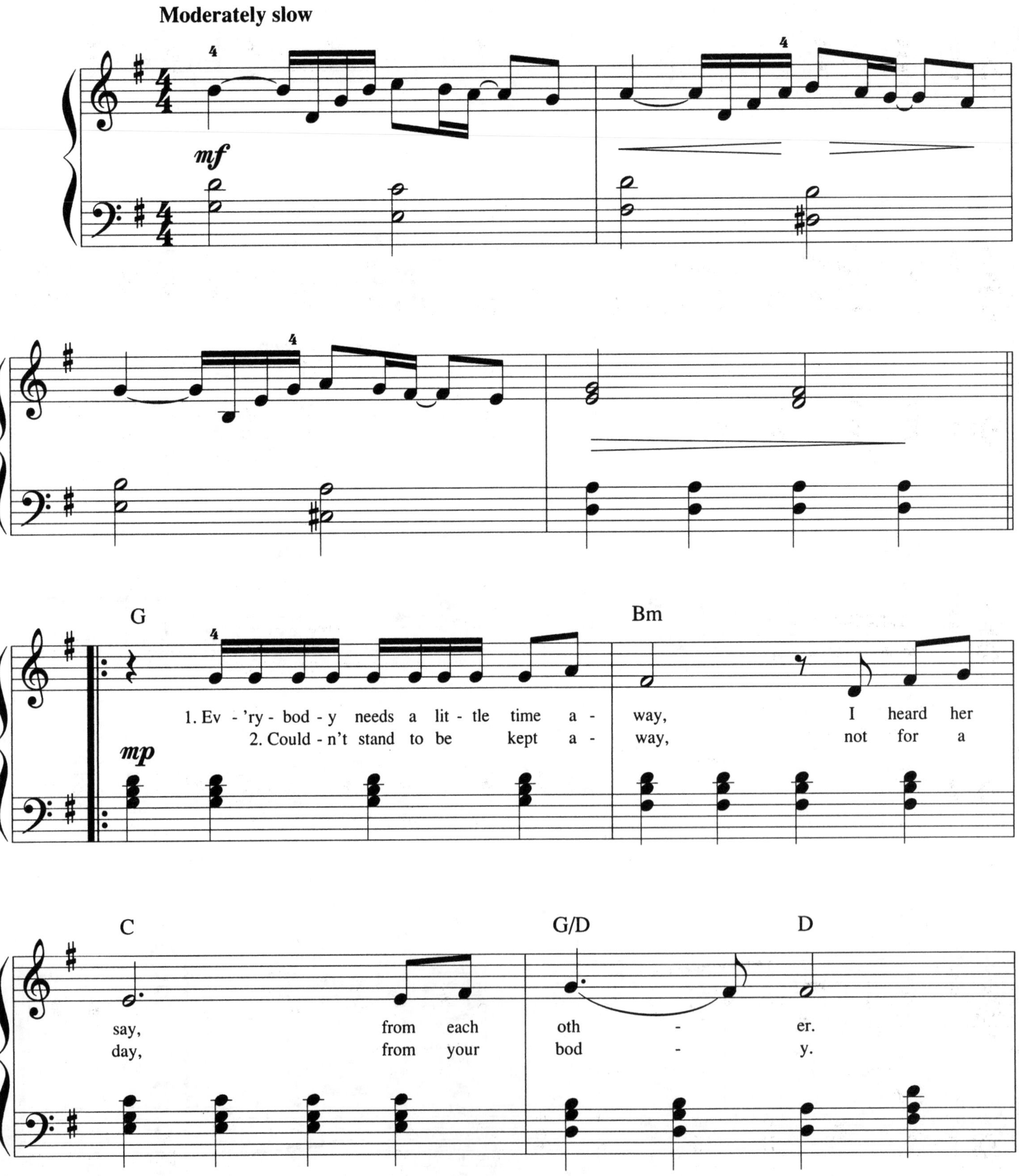

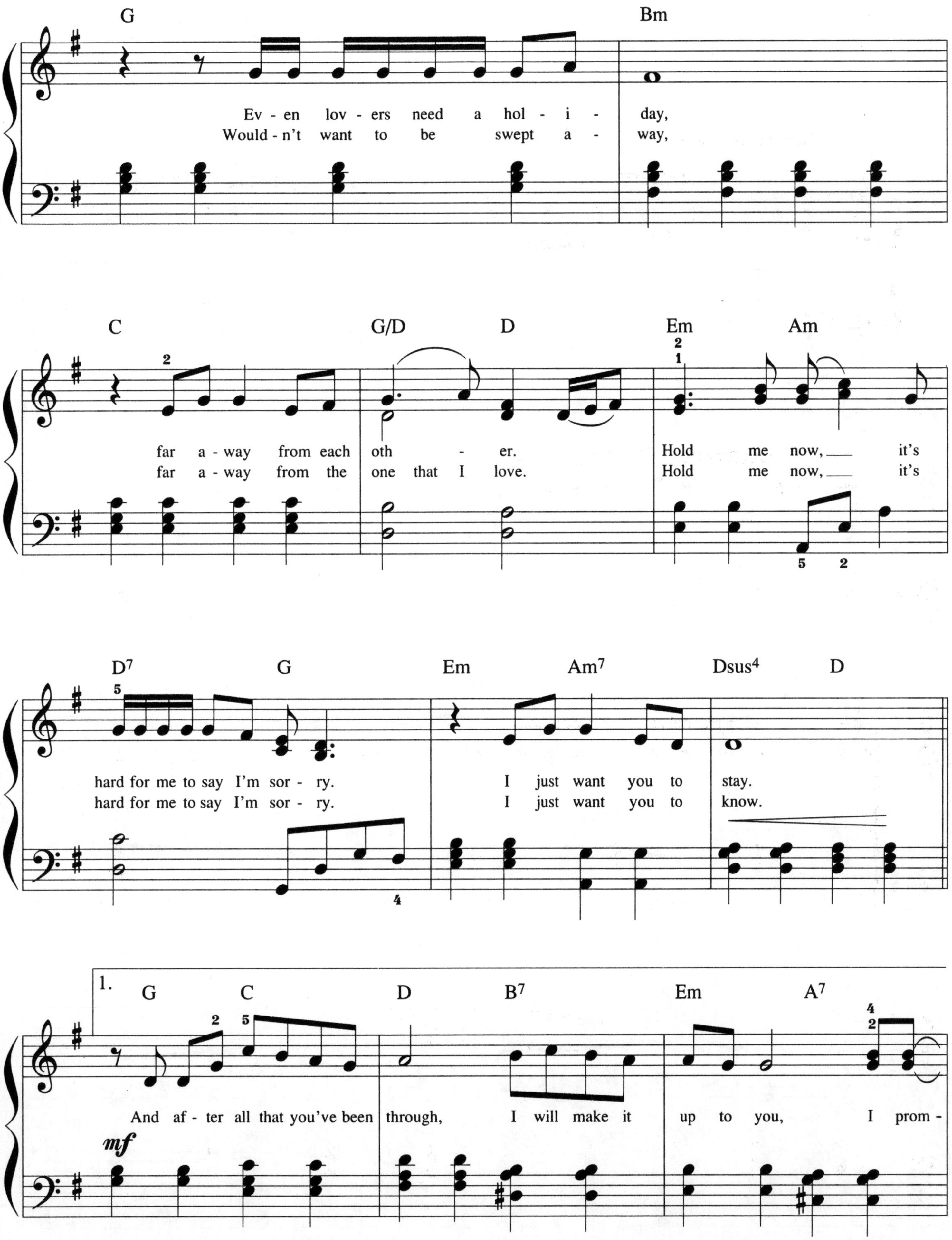
G
Bm
Ev - en lov - ers need a hol - i - day,
Would - n't want to be swept a - way,
C
G/D
D
Em
Am
far a - way from each oth - er.
far a - way from the one that I love.
Hold me now, it's
Hold me now, it's
D7
G
Em
Am7
Dsus4
D
hard for me to say I'm sor - ry.
hard for me to say I'm sor - ry.
I just want you to stay.
I just want you to know.
1.
G
C
D
B7
Em
A7
And af - ter all that you've been through,
I will make it up to you, I prom -
mf

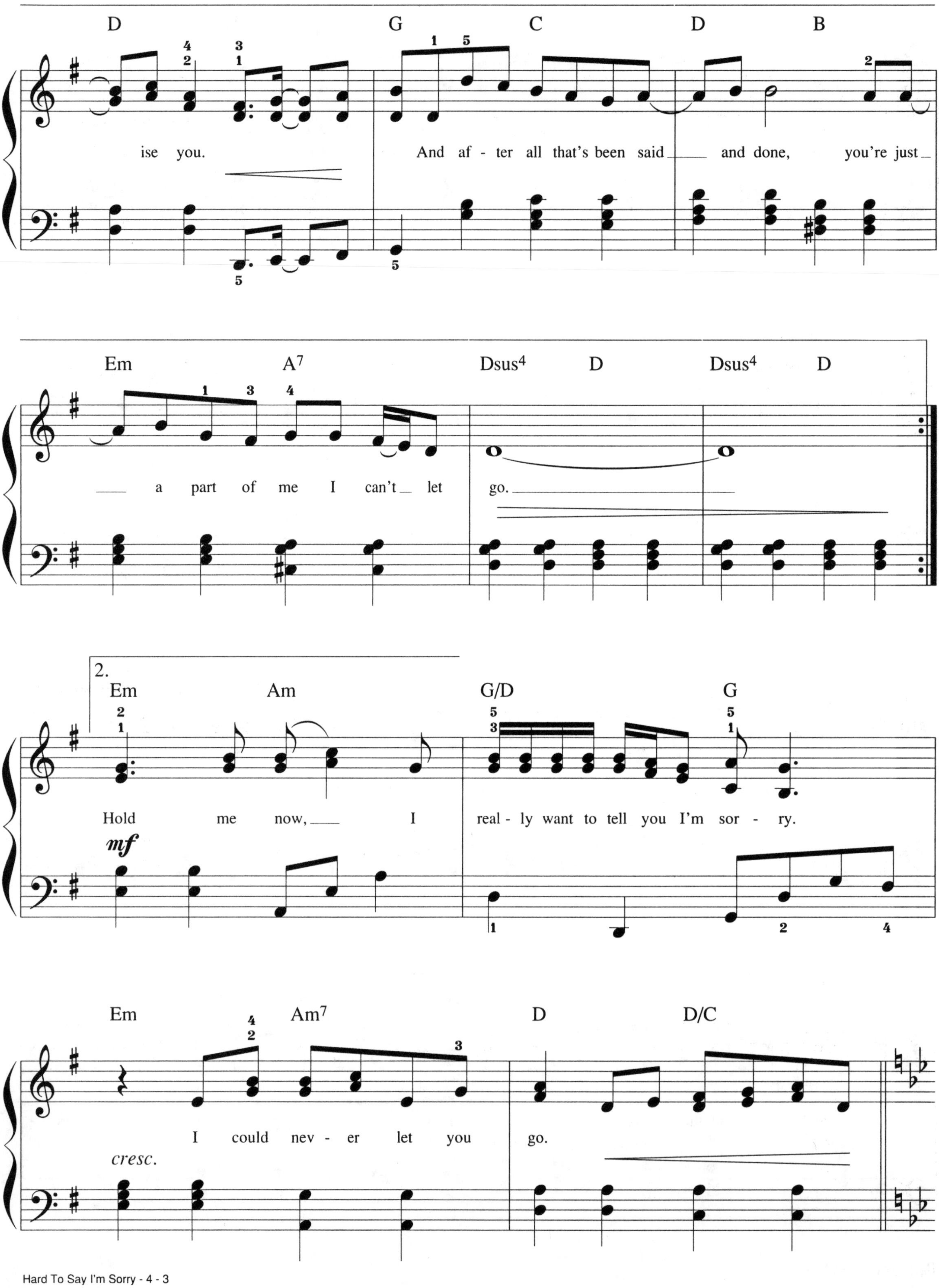
D G C D B
ise you. And af - ter all that's been said and done, you're just
Em A7 Dsus4 D Dsus4 D
a part of me I can't let go.
2.
Em Am G/D G
Hold me now, I real - ly want to tell you I'm sor - ry.
mf
Em Am7 D D/C
I could nev - er let you go.
cresc.

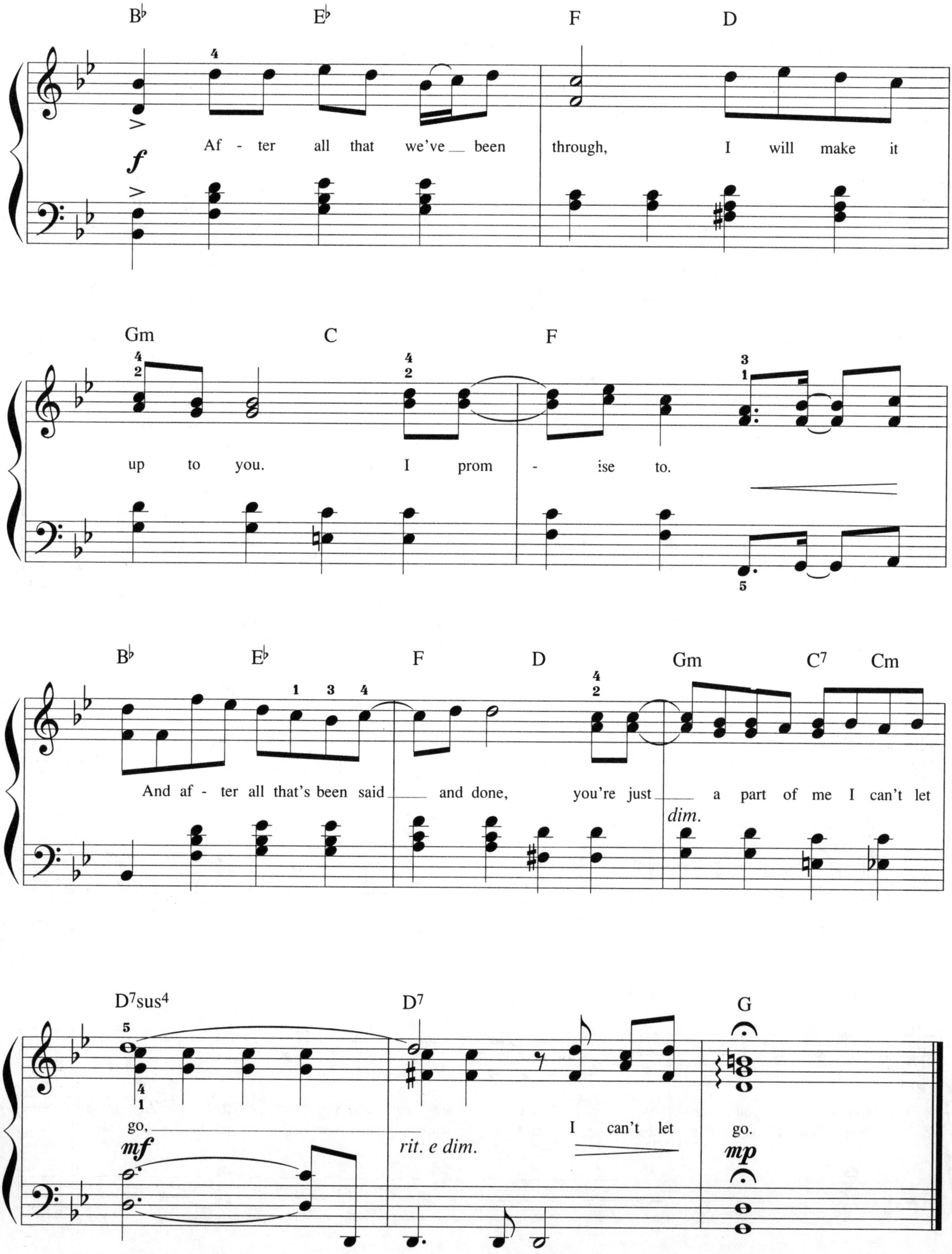
B♭ E♭ F D
After all that we've been through, I will make it
f
Gm C F
up to you. I promise to.
B♭ E♭ F D Gm C7 Cm
And after all that's been said and done, you're just a part of me I can't let
dim.
D7sus4 D7 G
go, I can't let go.
mf
rit. e dim.
mp

From the Twentieth Century Fox Motion Picture "ONE FINE DAY"

FOR THE FIRST TIME

Words and Music by
JAMES NEWTON HOWARD,
ALLAN RICH and JUD FRIEDMAN
Arranged by DAN COATES

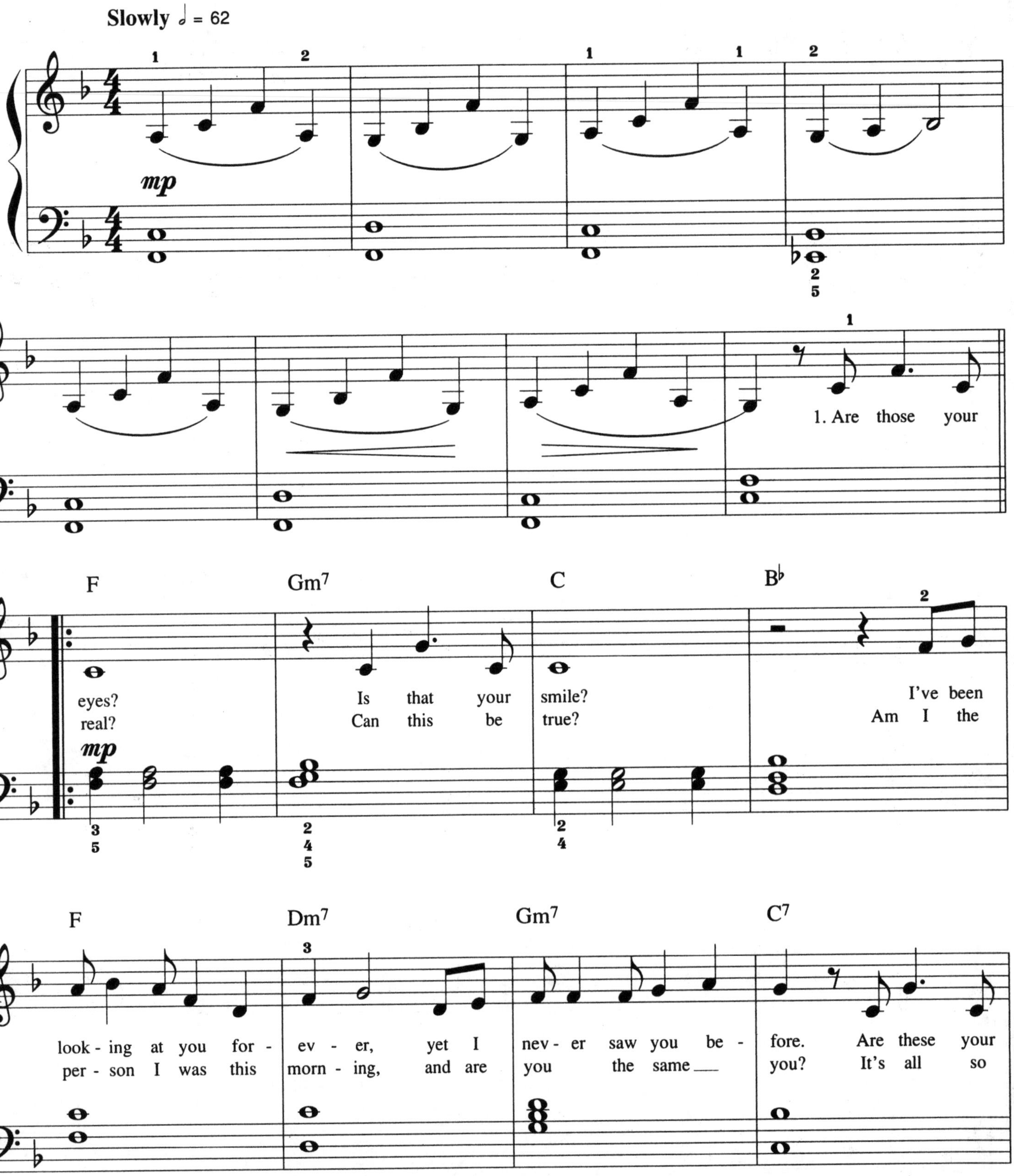

F
B♭
F/A
B♭
hands hold - ing mine? Now I
strange. How can it be? All a -
Dm
B♭
Csus4
C
won - der how I could - 've been so blind.
long this love was right in front of me.
And for the
F
B♭
Dm
C/E
first time, I am look - ing in your eyes. For the
mf
F
B♭
Csus4
C
first time I'm see - ing who you are. I can't be -

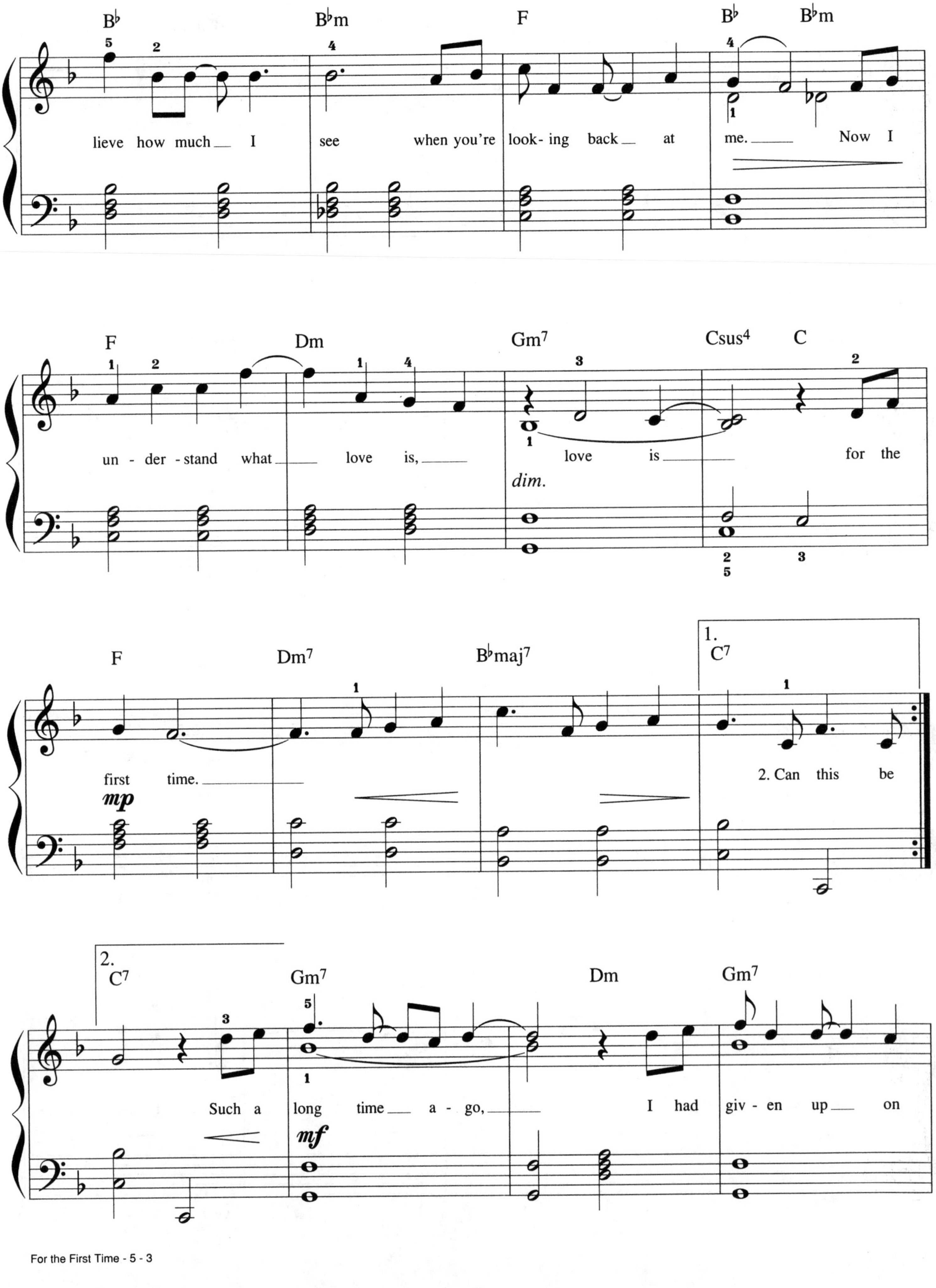
B♭ B♭m F B♭ B♭m
lieve how much I see when you're look-ing back at me. Now I
F Dm Gm7 Csus4 C
un - der - stand what love is, love is for the
dim.
F Dm7 B♭maj7 1. C7
first time. 2. Can this be
mp
2. C7 Gm7 Dm Gm7
Such a long time a - go, I had giv - en up on
mf

C7 F C Dm
finding this emotion ever again.
F/C Bm7(♭5) E7sus4
But you're here with me now, yes, I found you somehow,
f
E7 Am Dsus4 D
and I've never been so sure. And for the
dim.
G C Em D/F♯
first time, I am looking in your eyes. For the
mf

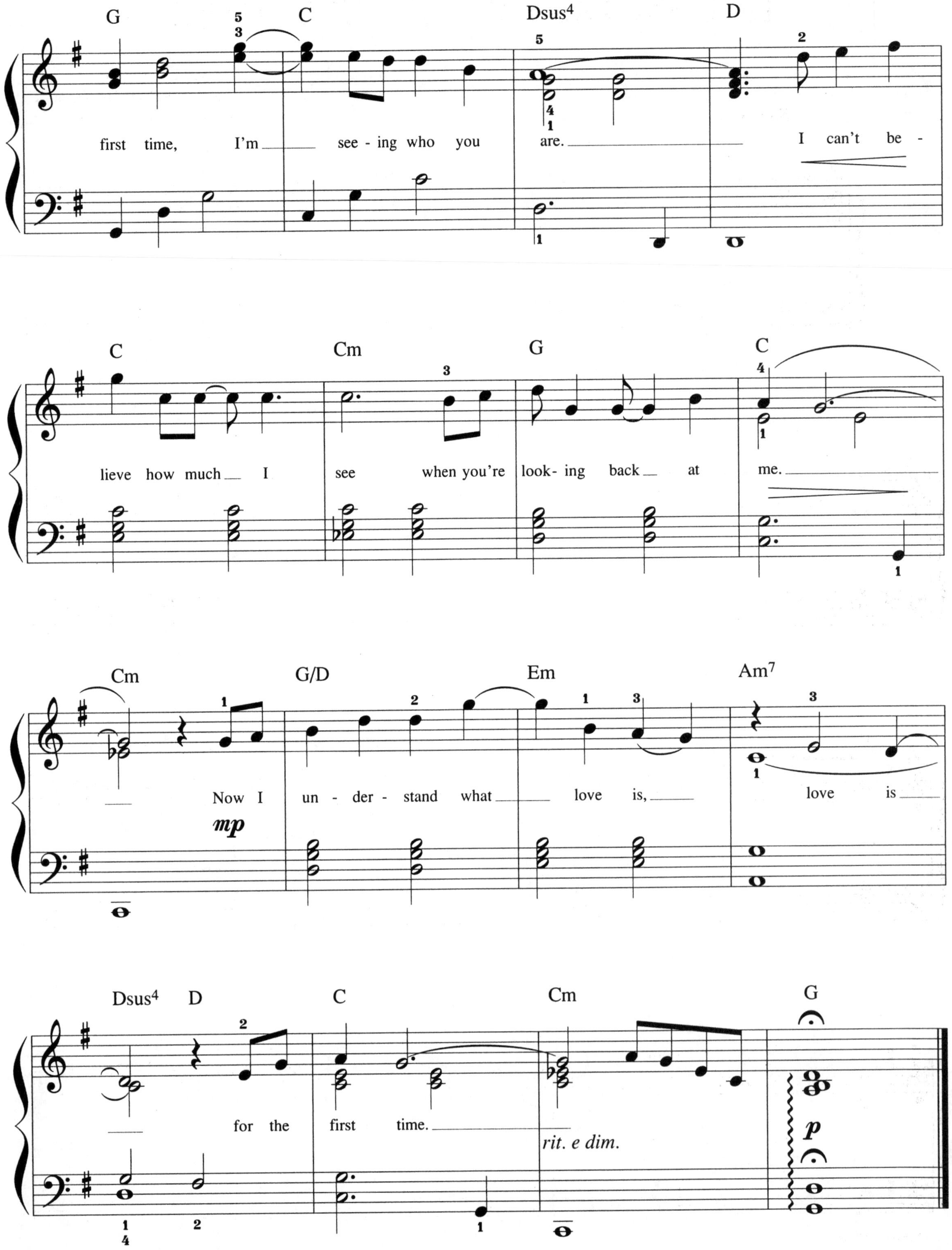
G C Dsus4 D
first time, I'm see - ing who you are. I can't be -
C Cm G C
lieve how much I see when you're look- ing back at me.
Cm G/D Em Am7
Now I un - der - stand what love is, love is
mp
Dsus4 D C Cm G
for the first time.
rit. e dim.
p

IF TOMORROW NEVER COMES

Words and Music by
KENT BLAZY and GARTH BROOKS
Arranged by DAN COATES

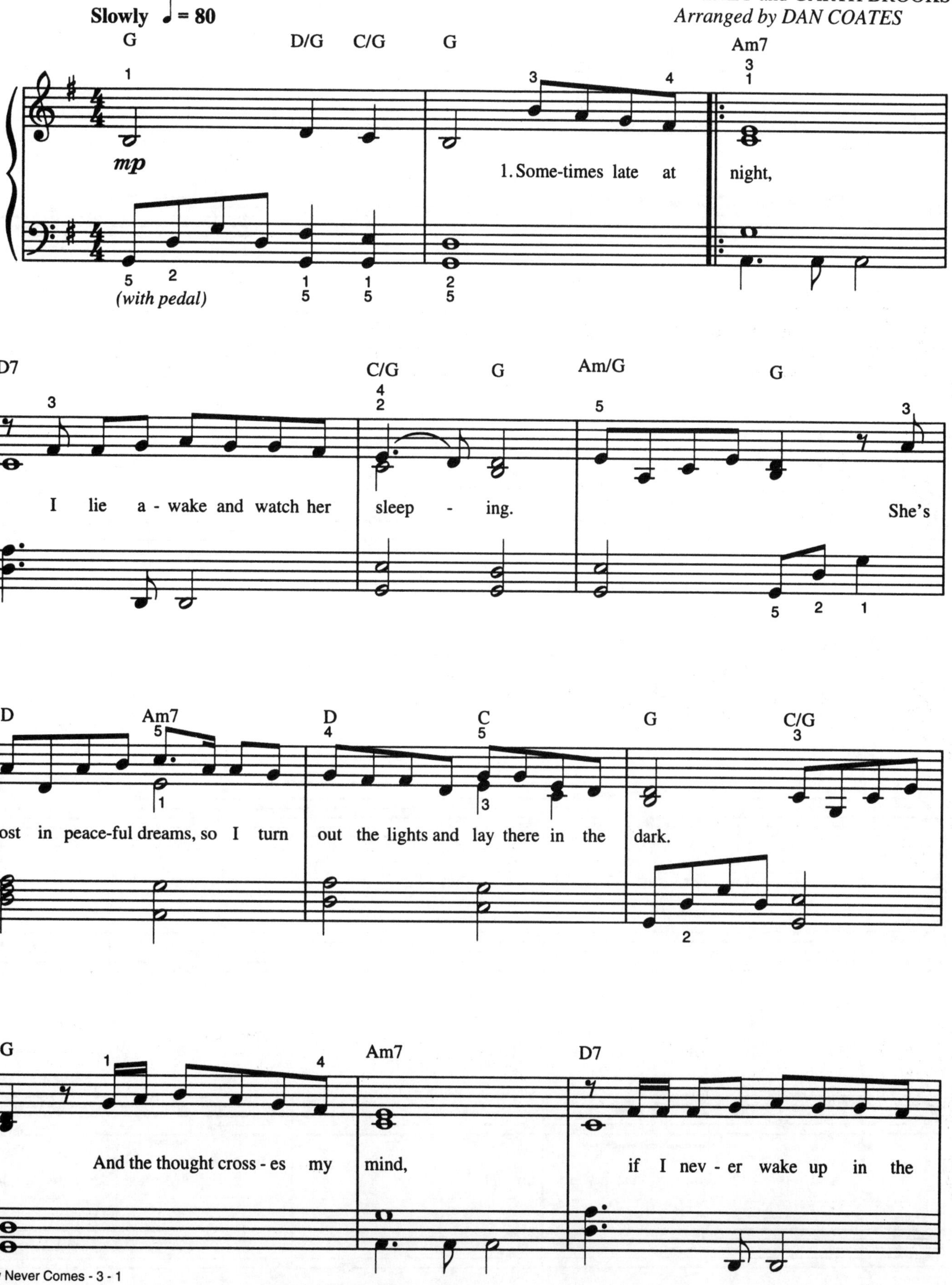

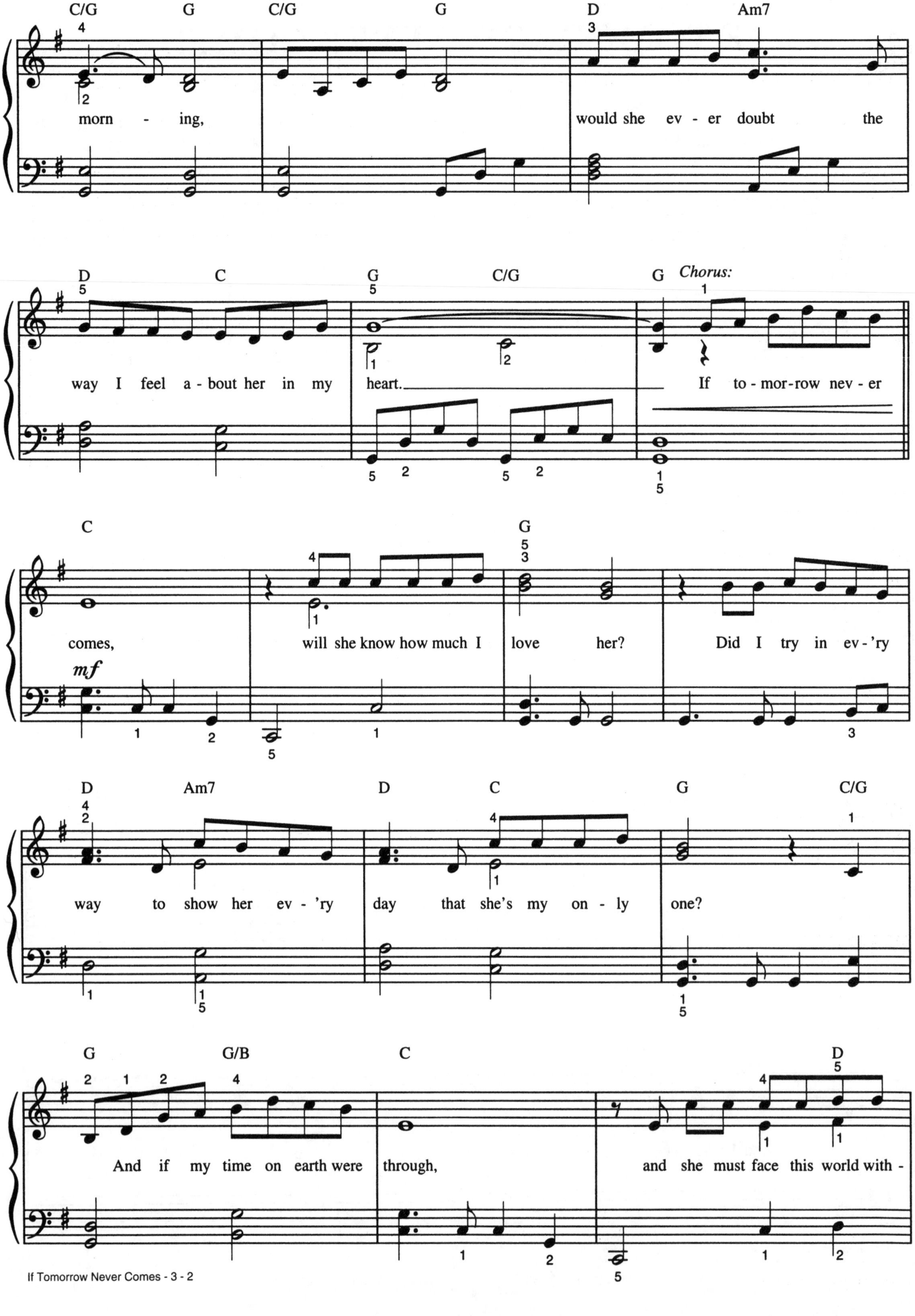
C/G G C/G G D Am7
morn - ing, would she ev - er doubt the
D C G C/G G
Chorus:
way I feel a - bout her in my heart. If to - mor-row nev - er
C G
comes, will she know how much I love her? Did I try in ev - 'ry
mf
D Am7 D C G C/G
way to show her ev - 'ry day that she's my on - ly one?
G G/B C D
And if my time on earth were through, and she must face this world with -

Verse 2:
'Cause I've lost loved ones in my life
Who never knew how much I loved them.
Now I live with the regret
That my true feelings for them never were revealed.
So I made a promise to myself
To say each day how much she means to me
And avoid the circumstance
Where there's no second chance
To tell her how I feel. 'Cause... *(To Chorus:)*

From the Motion Picture "THE PREACHER'S WIFE"

I BELIEVE IN YOU AND ME

Words and Music by
SANDY LINZER and DAVID WOLFERT
Arranged by DAN COATES

Am7
Gm7
C7
me. Oh, yes, you will. And I be - lieve in
F
F7
B♭maj7
dreams a - gain. I be - lieve that love will nev - er end. And like the riv - er finds the
mf
B♭m7
E♭7
F/C
Am7
Dm7
sea, I was lost, now I'm free, 'cause
Gm7
B♭/C
1. F
B♭/C
I be - lieve in you and me. 2. I will nev - er

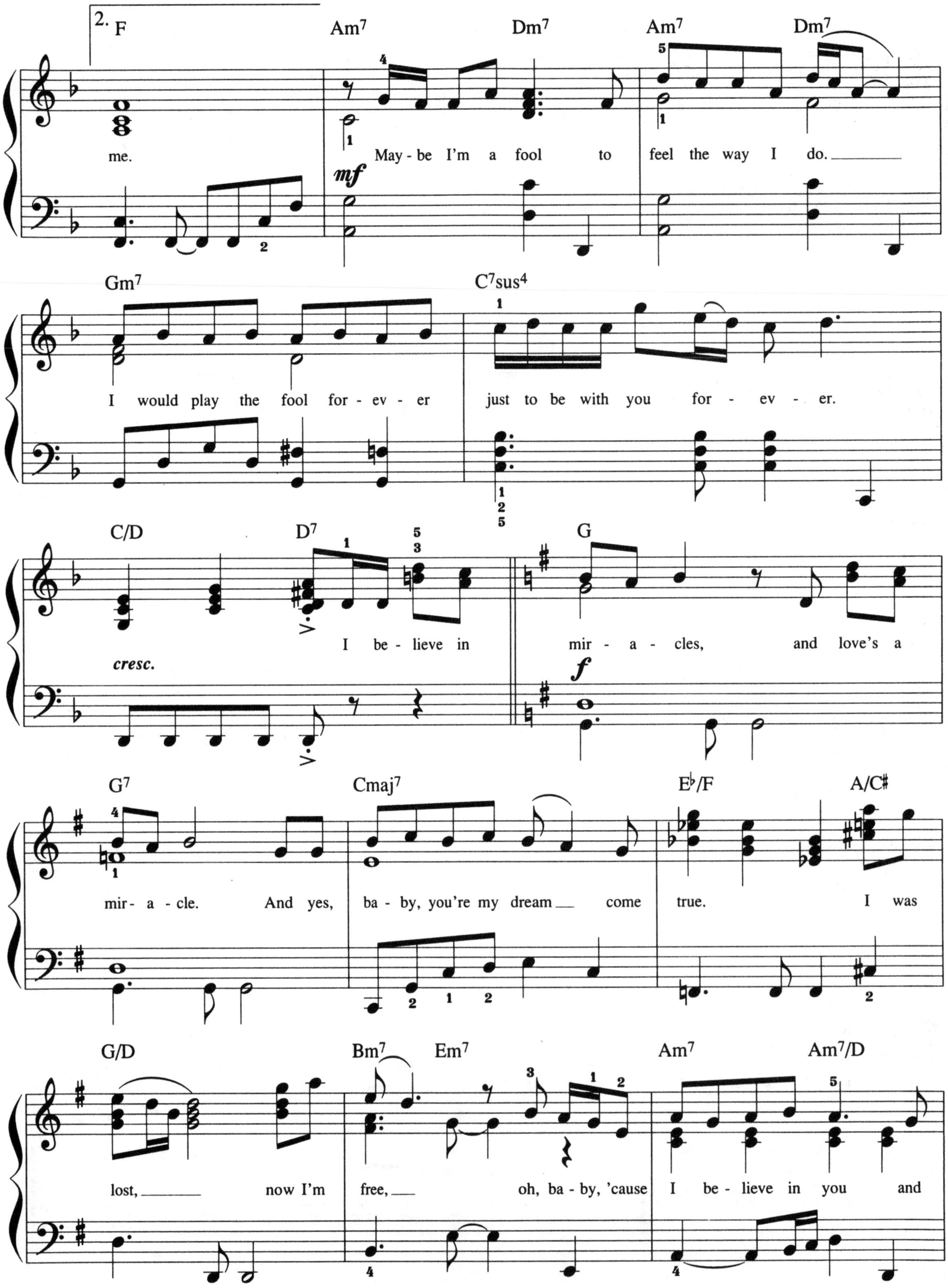
2.
F Am7 Dm7 Am7 Dm7
me. May - be I'm a fool to feel the way I do.
mf
Gm7 C7sus4
I would play the fool for - ev - er just to be with you for - ev - er.
C/D D7 G
I be - lieve in mir - a - cles, and love's a
cresc.
f
G7 Cmaj7 E♭/F A/C♯
mir - a - cle. And yes, ba - by, you're my dream come true. I was
G/D Bm7 Em7 Am7 Am7/D
lost, now I'm free, oh, ba - by, 'cause I be - lieve in you and

Verse 2:
I will never leave your side,
I will never hurt your pride.
When all the chips are down,
I will always be around
Just to be right where you are, my love.
Oh, I love you, boy.
I will never leave you out,
I will always let you in
To places no one has ever been.
Deep inside, can't you see?
I believe in you and me.

ALWAYS BE MY BABY

Words and Music by
MANUEL SEAL, JERMAINE DUPRI
and MARIAH CAREY
Arranged by DAN COATES

F C Dm7 Am
Now you want to be free, so I'll let you fly.
But in - ev - i - ta - bly, you'll be back a - gain.
B♭ Gm7 C7
'Cause I know in my heart, babe, our love will nev - er die, no.
'Cause you know in your heart, babe, our love will nev - er end, no.
F F/A B♭maj7 C7 C♯dim7
You'll al - ways be a part of me, I'm part of you in - def - i - nite - ly.
mf
Dm F/A B♭maj7 C7
Boy, don't you know you can't es - cape me, ooh, dar - ling, 'cause you'll al - ways be my

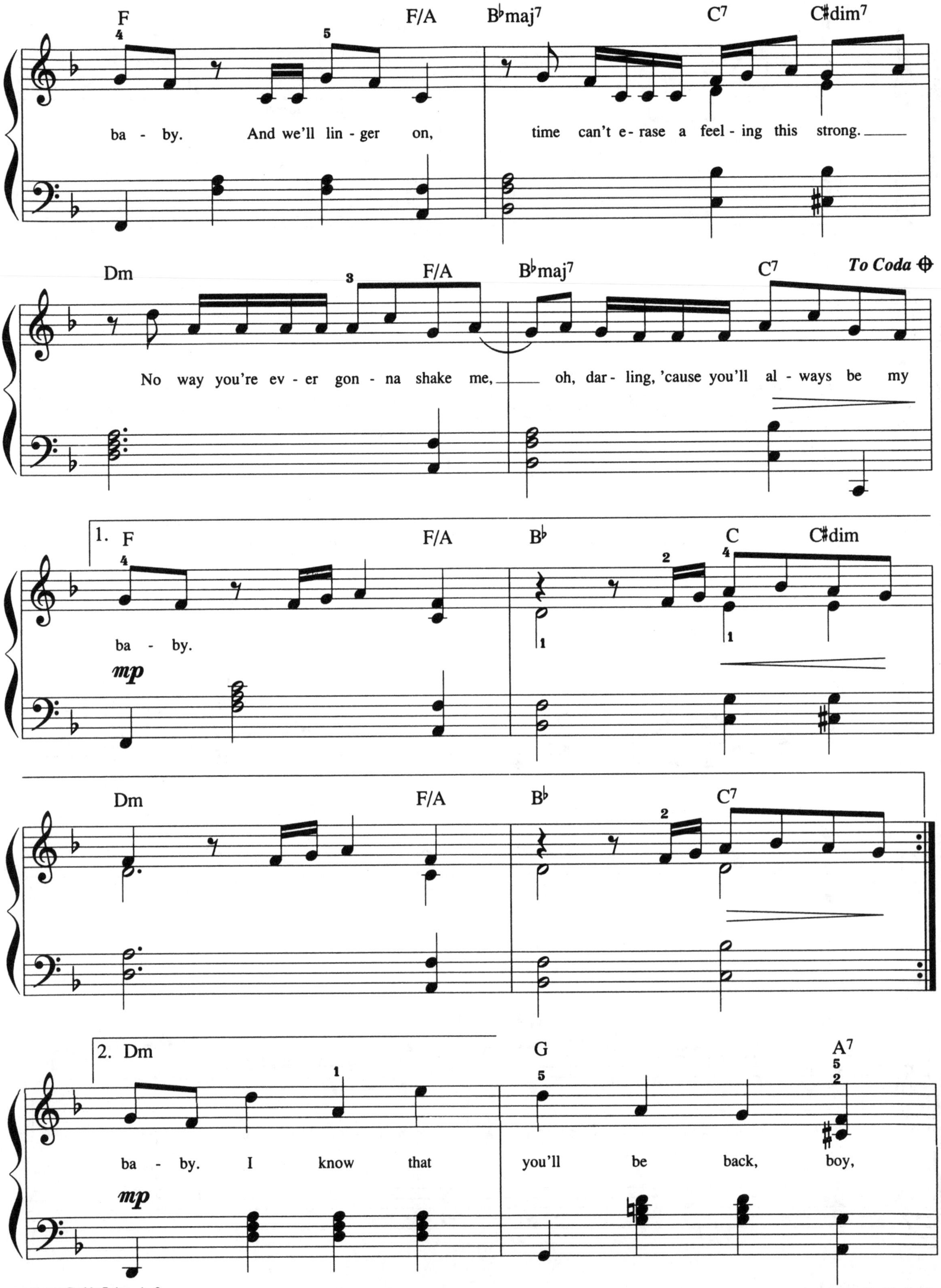
F F/A B♭maj7 C7 C♯dim7
ba - by. And we'll lin - ger on, time can't e - rase a feel - ing this strong.
Dm F/A B♭maj7 C7
To Coda
No way you're ev - er gon - na shake me, oh, dar - ling, 'cause you'll al - ways be my
1. F F/A B♭ C C♯dim
ba - by.
mp
Dm F/A B♭ C7
2. Dm G A7
ba - by. I know that you'll be back, boy,
mp

B♭
when your days and your nights get a lit - tle bit
Am7
cold - er.
cresc.
Dm
I know that
mf
G
you'll be right back.
A
Oh,
B♭
ba - by, be - lieve me, it's on - ly a mat - ter of
f
C7
time, time.
D.S. 𝄋 al Coda
Coda
F
ba - by.
mp
F/A
B♭
C
C♯dim
Dm
F/A
B♭
C7
rit. e dim.
F
p

MACARENA

Words and Music by
ANTONIO ROMERO and RAFAEL RUIZ
Arranged by DAN COATES

grí - a Ma - ca - re - na que tu
cuer - po‿es pa' dar - le‿a - le -
grí - a‿y co - sa - bue - na.
Da - le‿a tu cuer - po‿a - le -
grí - a Ma - ca - re - na,
eh, Ma - ca -
re - na. Ma - ca -
G
re - na tie - ne‿un no - vio que se
mp
lla - ma, que - se
lla - ma de‿a - pe - lli - do Vi - to -
ri - no. Y‿en la
ju - ra de ban - de - ra del mu -
cha - cho

C
se la dió con dos a - mi - gos. Ma - ca - re - na tie - ne‿un no - vio que se
mf
B♭
lla - ma, que se lla - ma de‿a - pe - lli - do Vi - to - ri - no y‿en la
A♭
D
ju - ra de ban - de - ra del mu - cha - cho se la dió con dos a -
1.
G
2.
G
mi - gos. mi - gos. Ma - ca - re - na, Ma - ca - re - na, Ma - ca -
re - na, que te gus - tan los ve - ra - nos de Mar - be - lla. Ma - ca -

re - na, Ma - ca - re - na, Ma - ca - re - na, que te gus - ta la mo - vi - da gue - rri - lle - ra.
G
Da - le‿a tu cuer - po‿a - le - grí - a Ma - ca - re - na que tu cuer - po‿es pa' dar - le‿a - le - grí - a‿y co - sa bue - na.
Da - le‿a tu cuer - po‿a - le - grí - a Ma - ca - re - na, eh, Ma - ca - re - na.
(Repeat twice)
Da - le‿a tu cuer - po‿a - le - grí - a Ma - ca - re - na, eh, Ma - ca - re - na!
f
sfz
8va
8vb

SEND ME A LOVER

Words and Music by
RICHARD HAHN and
GEORGE THATCHER
Arranged by DAN COATES

C
B♭
Dm
Csus4
C
this to be de - nied.
what I know is true.
on - ly my fear stands in our
I'm in - to you in ev - 'ry
way.
way.
cresc.
F
Fmaj7
Send me a lov - er,
some - one to be - lieve in.
mf
F7
B♭
Please send me some - one that I can
hold.
F
Am
Send me a lov - er,
a new be - gin - ning,

Cm
B♭ E♭ B♭
some - one to take a - way the cold and give me
To Coda ⊕
D♭ F/C Bm7(♭5) B♭ C7
back what I've been miss - ing, all the love that waits in - side your
1. F
2. F
heart.
mp
heart.
Am7 B♭
I thought that love was on - ly a word I'd nev - er feel, all the
mf

Dm
B♭
Dm7
pas - sion I hold in - side was just a dream.
Am7
B♭
But out of your heart you spoke to me all that I'd im - ag - ine, and I've
Gm7
Csus4
C
D.S. al Coda
fall - en so in love with you.
Coda
F
B♭
F/A
Gm7
C7
F
heart, all the love that waits in - side your heart.
mp
dim. e rit.

From the Lucasfilm Ltd. Productions "STAR WARS", "THE EMPIRE STRIKES BACK" and "RETURN OF THE JEDI" - Twentieth Century-Fox Releases.

STAR WARS
(Main Theme)

Music by
JOHN WILLIAMS
Arranged by DAN COATES

C/D
mf
D
Cm/A
ff
D
sfz
G
Gmaj7
C
G
C
G
mf
F
D
G
Gmaj7
C
G
E♭
D
G
sfz
f

From the Twentieth Century-Fox Motion Picture

THAT THING YOU DO!

Words and Music by
ADAM SCHLESINGER
Arranged by DAN COATES

C F G Am
cruel. You nev - er ev - en knew a - bout the
D F G
heart - ache I've been go - in' through. Well, I
cresc.
To Coda
Am D C C7
try and try to for - get you, girl but it's just so hard to
f
F Fm C Fm C
do. Ev - 'ry time you do that thing you do.

1. G7
2. C
mf
F
I don't ask a - lot, girl, but I
f
Am
know one thing's for sure.
It's your
D
love I have - n't got, girl and I
D.S. 𝄋 al Coda
G7
just can't take it
A♭7
an - y - more.
G7
ff

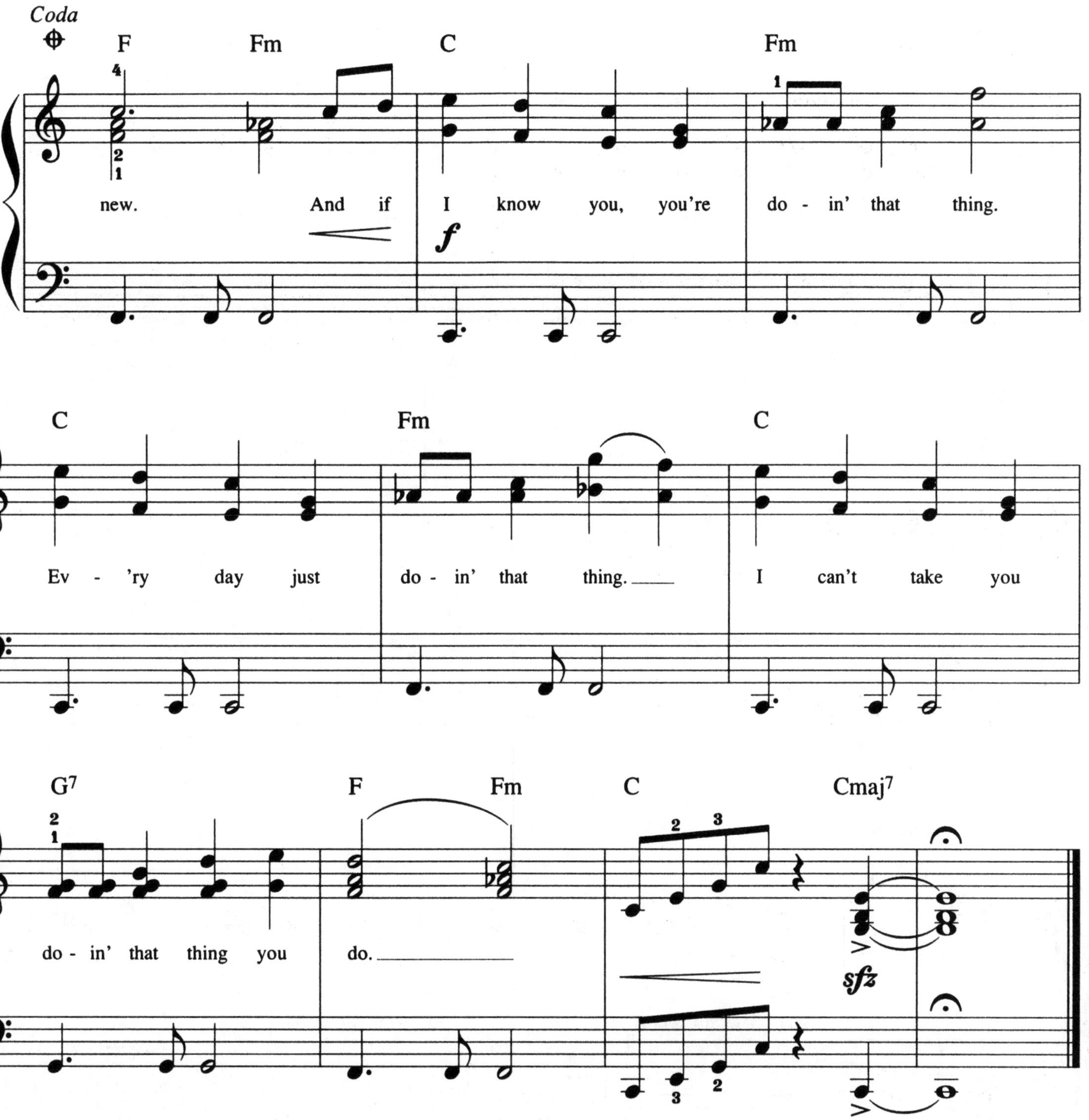

Verse 2:
I know all the games you play.
And I'm gonna find a way to let you know
That you'll be mine someday.
'Cause we could be happy, can't you see?
If you'd only let me be the one to hold you
And keep you here with me.
'Cause I try and try to forget you, girl,
But it's just too hard to do.
Every time you do that thing you do.

Verse 3:
(8 Bar Instrumental Solo...)
'Cause we could be happy, can't you see?
If you'd only let me be the one to hold you
And keep you here with me.
'Cause it hurts me so just to see you go
Around with someone new.
(To Coda:)

VALENTINE

Composed by
JIM BRICKMAN and JACK KUGELL
Arranged by DAN COATES

Moderately slow (♩ = 92)

B♭ C7 F/A
in - side, I'd still feel for you. And e - ven if the sun
mf
B♭ C Am7 F/A B♭ C
re - fused to shine, e - ven if ro - mance ran out of rhyme,
Gm7 A7sus4 A7 Dm F/C
you would still have my heart un - til the end of time.
To Coda
Bm7(♭5) F/C B♭/C C
You're all I need, my love,
'Cause all I need is you,
my Val - en -

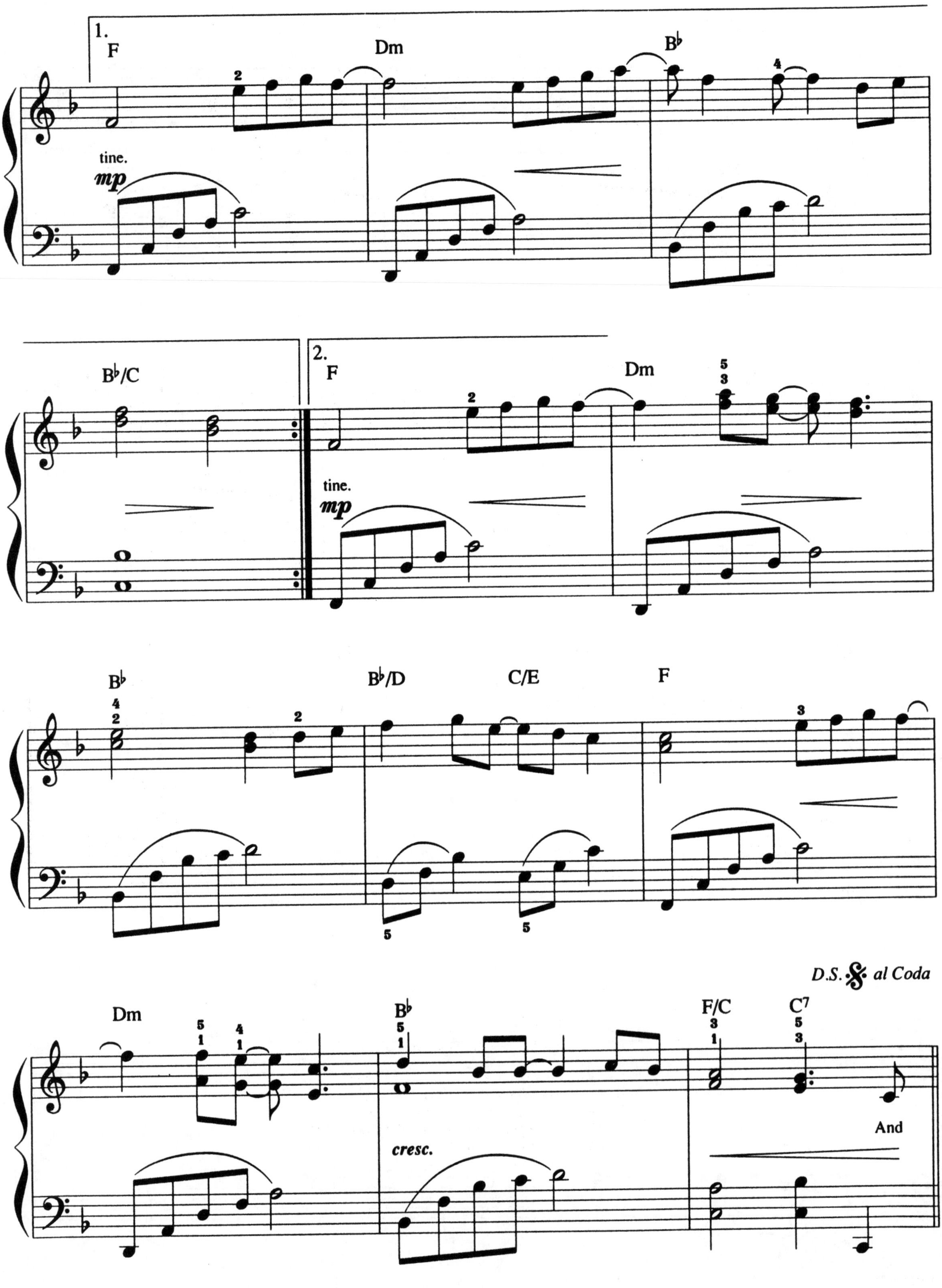
1.
F
Dm
B♭
tine.
mp
B♭/C
2.
F
Dm
tine.
mp
B♭
B♭/D
C/E
F
D.S. al Coda
Dm
B♭
cresc.
F/C
C7
And

Verse 2:
All of my life,
I have been waiting for all you give to me.
You've opened my eyes
And shown me how to love unselfishly.
I've dreamed of this a thousand times before,
But in my dreams I couldn't love you more.
I will give you my heart until the end of time.
You're all I need, my love,
My Valentine.

UNTIL I FIND YOU AGAIN

Music and Lyrics by
RICHARD MARX
Arranged by DAN COATES

F
Dm
Gsus4
G
of tears, my heart's got no room left in - side.
for you. Your mem - 'ry just won't let me go.
cresc.
C
F/C
G/C
How man - y dreams will end?
How long can I pre - tend?
mf
C
Am
Dm
How man - y times will love pass me by un -
To Coda
1.
2.
C/G
G
F
C
C
til I find you a - gain?
gain?

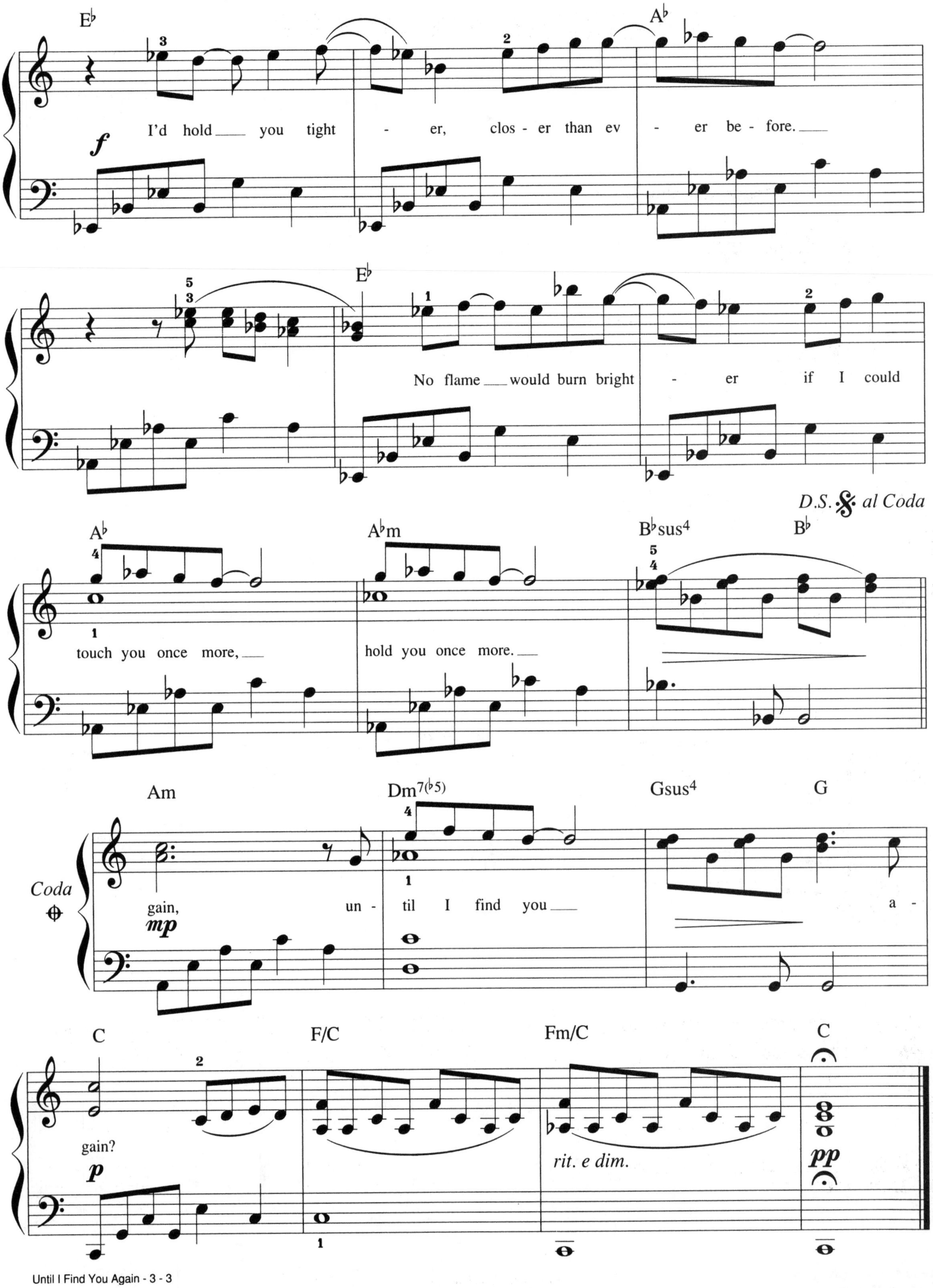
E♭
A♭
f
I'd hold you tight - er, clos - er than ev - er be - fore.
E♭
No flame would burn bright - er if I could
D.S. 𝄋 al Coda
A♭
A♭m
B♭sus4
B♭
touch you once more,
hold you once more.
Am
Dm7(♭5)
Gsus4
G
Coda
gain, un - til I find you a -
mp
C
F/C
Fm/C
C
gain?
p
rit. e dim.
pp

UN-BREAK MY HEART

Words and Music by
DIANE WARREN
Arranged by DAN COATES

A F♯ Bm
take these tears a - way. I need your arms to
kiss this pain a - way. I can't for - get the
Em7 A Bm
hold me now. Nights are so un - kind. Bring back those nights
day you left. Time is so un - kind. Life is so cruel
Em7 A A7
when I held you be - side me.
with - out you here be - side me.
Un - break my
Dm Gm7 C
heart, say you love me a - gain.
mf

A7 Dm Gm7
Un - do this hurt you caused when you walked out the door and walked
C A7 Dm
out of my life. Un - cry these tears I
Gm7 C To Coda A7 C/B♭ B♭
cried so man - y nights. Un - break my heart.
1. A F♯7
dim.

2.
A
F♯7
Bm
cresc.
f
Don't leave me in
Em
A
all this pain,
don't leave me out in the rain.
Bm
Em
A
A7
D.S. 𝄋 al Coda
Bring back those nights when I held you be - side me.
Un - break my
Coda
A7
Dm
Gm7
Un - break my,
un - break my heart, sweet ba - by.
f

C A7 Dm
Come back and say you love me. Un - break my
Gm7 C A7 Dm
heart, sweet dar - ling. With - out you, I just can't go on.
Gm7 C A7 Dm
mf
Gm7 C A7 Dm(add9)
mp rit.

Music for Easy Piano
from
Dan Coates

30 Favorite TV Hits
(AF9635)

Titles include: Ashokan Farewell ("The Civil War") • Beverly Hills, 90210 (Main Theme) • I'll Be There for You ("Friends") • Jeopardy Theme • L.A. Law (Main Title Theme) • Linus and Lucy ("Peanuts" Special) • Love and Marriage ("Married with Children") • Theme from "Chicago Hope" • Theme from "Murder One" and more.

30 Great Country Songs
(AF9637)

Titles in this 30-song folio include: Angels Among Us • The Dance • Desperado • Forever's As Far As I'll Go • I Cross My Heart • I Swear • I Will Always Love You • If Tomorrow Never Comes • In This Life • The Keeper of the Stars • The River • Singing the Blues.

30 Popular Love Songs
(AF9634)

Titles include: All the Man That I Need • Always • Dreaming of You • For Your Love • Forever • Have You Ever Really Loved a Woman? • (Everything I Do) I Do It for You • I Swear • I Will Always Love You • More Than Words • The Rose • Tonight I Celebrate My Love for You • The Wind Beneath My Wings and others.

Because You Loved Me & Other Hot Pop Singles
(AF9674)

Titles include: Always Be My Baby (Mariah Carey) • Angel Eyes (Jim Brickman) • Because You Loved Me (Celine Dion) • Breakfast at Tiffany's (Deep Blue Something) • Exhale (Shoop Shoop) (Whitney Houston) • Have You Ever Really Loved a Woman (Bryan Adams) • Reach (Gloria Estefan) • One of Us (Joan Osborne) and more.

The Best of Jim Brickman (arr. Dan Coates)
(AF9735)

The best songs from Jim Brickman's first three albums have been collected in this exceptional Easy Piano edition. Titles are: Angel Eyes • Borders • By Heart • Heartland • Hero's Dream • If You Believe • Picture This • Rocket to the Moon • Shaker Lakes • Valentine.

The Best of the Eagles
(AF9556)

Dan Coates offers 12 of the Eagles' biggest hits in his popular Easy Piano arrangements. Titles include: The Best of My Love • Desperado • Heartache Tonight • Hotel California • I Can't Tell You Why • Love Will Keep Us Alive • Lyin' Eyes • New Kid in Town • One of These Nights • Peaceful Easy Feeling • Take It Easy • Take It to the Limit.

The Best in Country Sheet Music
(AF9701)

The biggest country hits from Garth Brooks, LeAnn Rimes, Shania Twain, Clint Black, John Michael Montgomery, Alabama, Vince Gill, and more. Titles include: Angels Among Us • Any Man of Mine • Blue • The Dance • Don't Take the Girl • Forever's As Far As I'll Go • I Can Love You Like That • I Cross My Heart • I Do • I Swear • I Will Always Love You • If Tomorrow Never Comes • In This Life • Long As I Live • The River • Unanswered Prayers • Years from Here • Your Love Amazes Me.

The Best in Popular Sheet Music
(AF9531A)

Dan Coates applies his popular easy piano arrangements to 25 of the hottest pop and country hits. Selections include: Angels Among Us • From a Distance • The Greatest Love of All • Have You Ever Really Loved a Woman? • I Swear • (Everything I Do) I Do It for You and more.

Biggest Hits of '95-'96
(AF9662)

Titles include: Because You Loved Me • Dreaming of You • Don't Turn Around • The Most Beautiful Girl in the World • Take a Bow • You Are Not Alone • Hold Me, Thrill Me, Kiss Me • One of Us • I Can Love You Like That • Somebody's Crying • The Sweetest Days • Have You Ever Really Loved a Woman? and more.

Dan Coates Easy Piano Collection (Pop, Country, Movie & TV Hits)
(AF9675)

Seventy-five of the most popular titles in music, including: Because You Loved Me • I Swear • Stairway to Heaven • The Keeper of the Stars • Angel Eyes • Your Cheatin' Heart • We're Off to See the Wizard • Up Where We Belong • Jeopardy Theme • Theme from "The Simpsons" and many more.

Fantastic TV & Movie Songs
(AF9525)

Here's an outstanding assortment of well-known television and movie melodies. Titles include: Beverly Hills 90210 (Main Theme) • How Do You Keep the Music Playing • (Everything I Do) I Do It for You • I Found Love • (Song from) M*A*S*H • The Pink Panther • The Rose • Singin' in the Rain • Theme from *New York, New York* and more.

Great Popular Music
(AF9506)

Songs include: Always • Everything I Do (I Do It for You) • From a Distance • The Greatest Love of All • I Swear • I Will Always Love You • Music Box Dancer • Over the Rainbow • The Rose • Theme from *Ice Castles* (Through the Eyes of Love) • The Wind Beneath My Wings and many more.

Great Popular Music, Volume II
(AF96100)

Continuing in this popular series is this collection of twenty big hits, arranged as only Dan Coates can, from pop to country and stage to screen. The titles include: Angel Eyes • Blue • Change the World • Dreaming of You • I Do • I'll Be There for You (Theme from "Friends") • Killing Me Softly (With His Song) • Reach • Send in the Clowns (From "A Little Night Music") • Stairway to Heaven • Tears in Heaven • Tomorrow.

Music from *The Star Wars Trilogy: Special Edition*
(0020B)

Music from the most popular films of all time. This book contains rare full-color photos from the revised editions of all three films. Titles are: Cantina Band • Princess Leia's Theme • Star Wars (Main Theme) • The Throne Room • The Imperial March • Ewok Celebration • Luke and Leia • Victory Celebration.

The Wizard of Oz
(AF9502)

Dan Coates applies his popular Easy Piano arrangements to the delightful score from this timeless movie classic. Here's a collector's item for players of all ages. Songs include: Ding-Dong! The Witch Is Dead • If Only I Had a Brain • If I Were the King of the Forest • Over the Rainbow • We're Off to See the Wizard and more.

WARNER BROS. PUBLICATIONS
15800 N.W. 48th Avenue • Miami, Florida 33014
A Warner Music Group Company